JOY OF JAPAN

Photo Story / Robert Ornig

hen you look at Japanese traditional
architecture, you have to look at Japanese
culture and its relationship with nature. You can
actually live in a harmonious, close contact with
nature — this very unique to Japan.
Tadao Ando

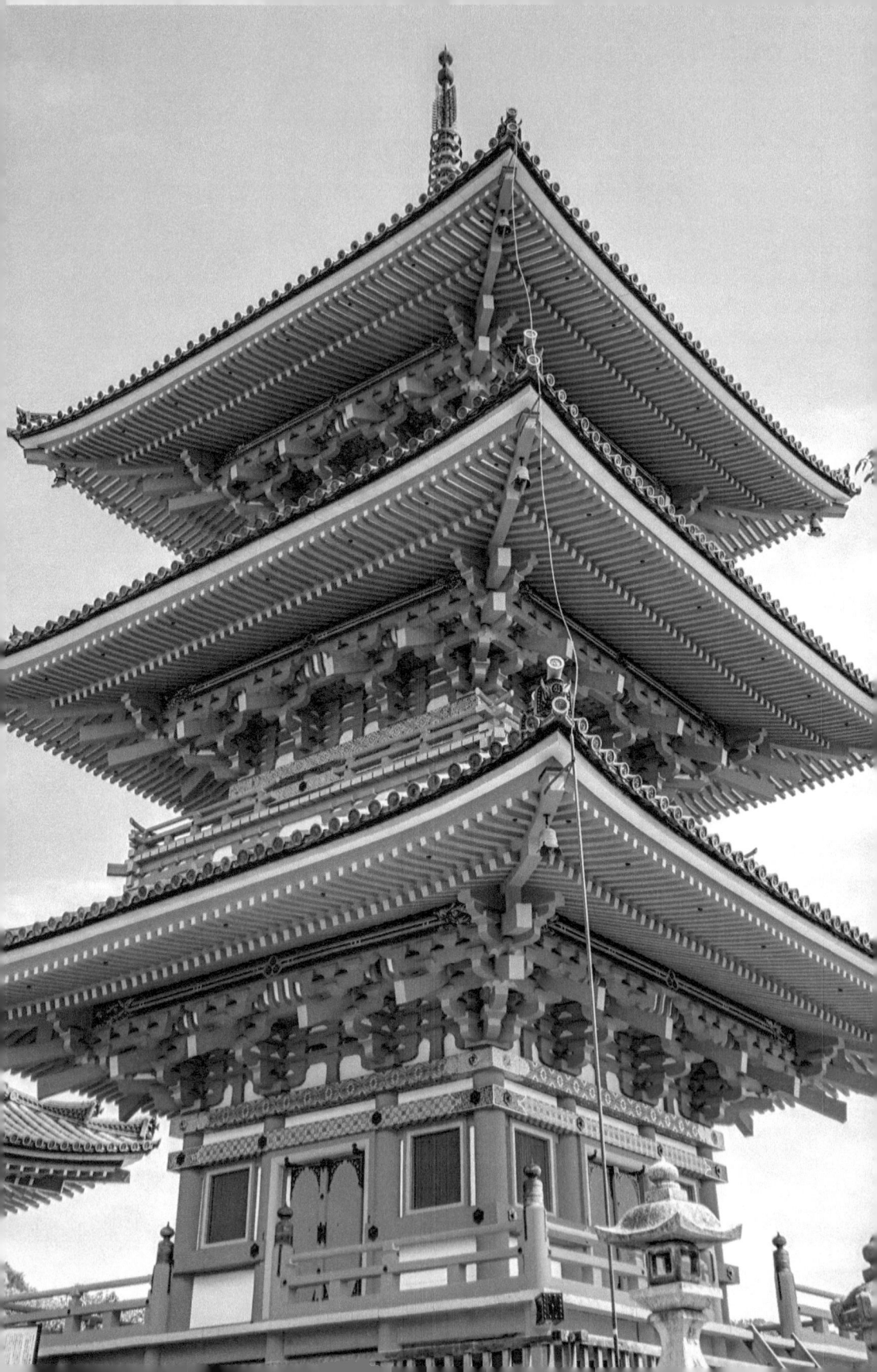

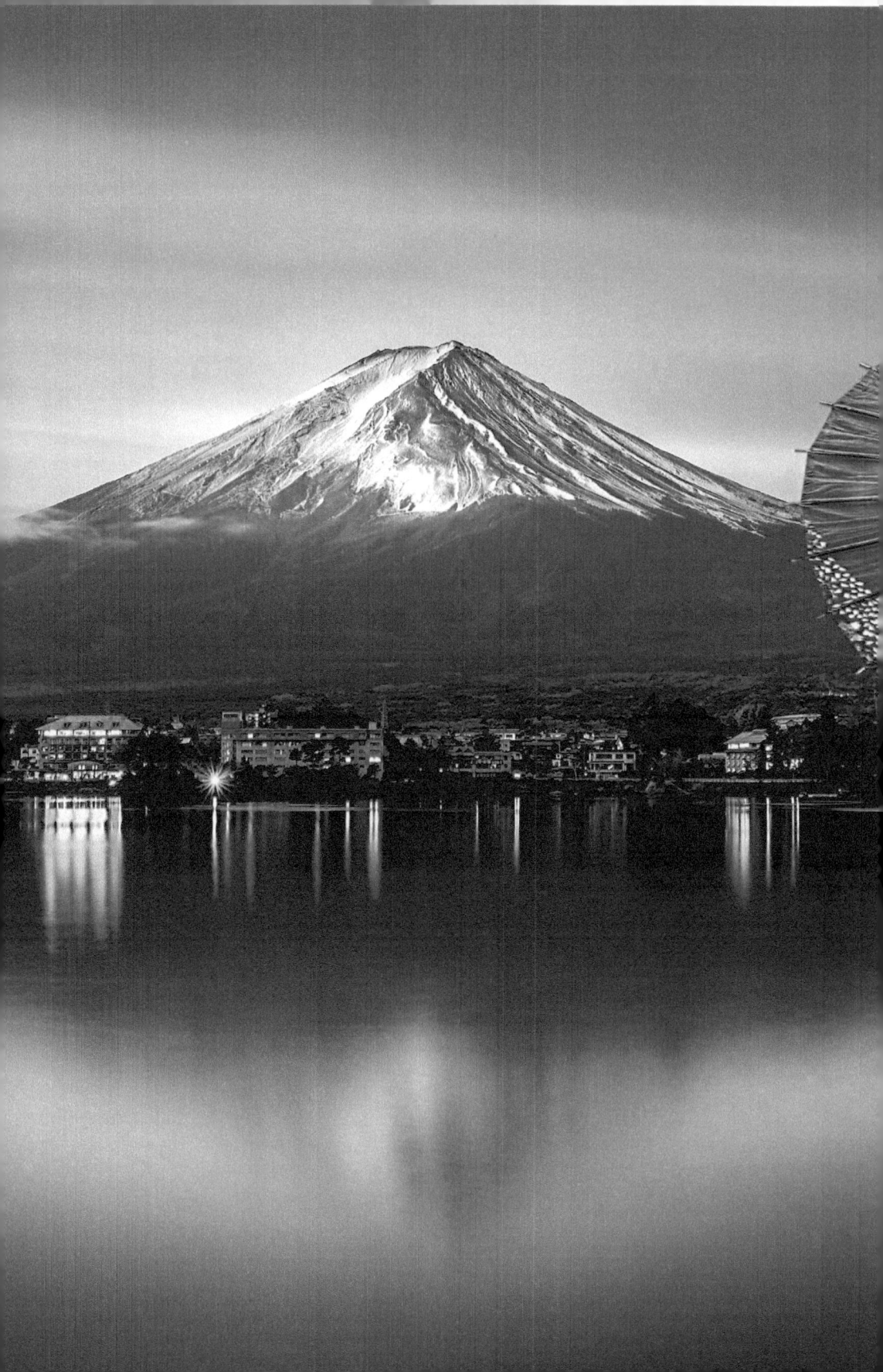

平成十六年九月吉日建之
平成二十年七月吉日建之
平成十八年三月吉日建之

松本市沖田一ノ八〇二八
東京都大田区
(株)ワークストア・トウキョウドク

東京
染谷裕之
清野貴経
齋藤 卓

愛知県丹羽郡扶桑町高雄

新潟県上越市上中田二七八
株式会社エム・エー・シ
代表取締役社長山口昭夫

和歌山県島越崎ノ丁
桜井市阿部七〇二
津田産実穂 濱田幸也
(株)夢工房

名古屋実業株

田中ミナ子 小林亜矢子
中山辰子 伊達弘子
三昧グループ 神谷昭男

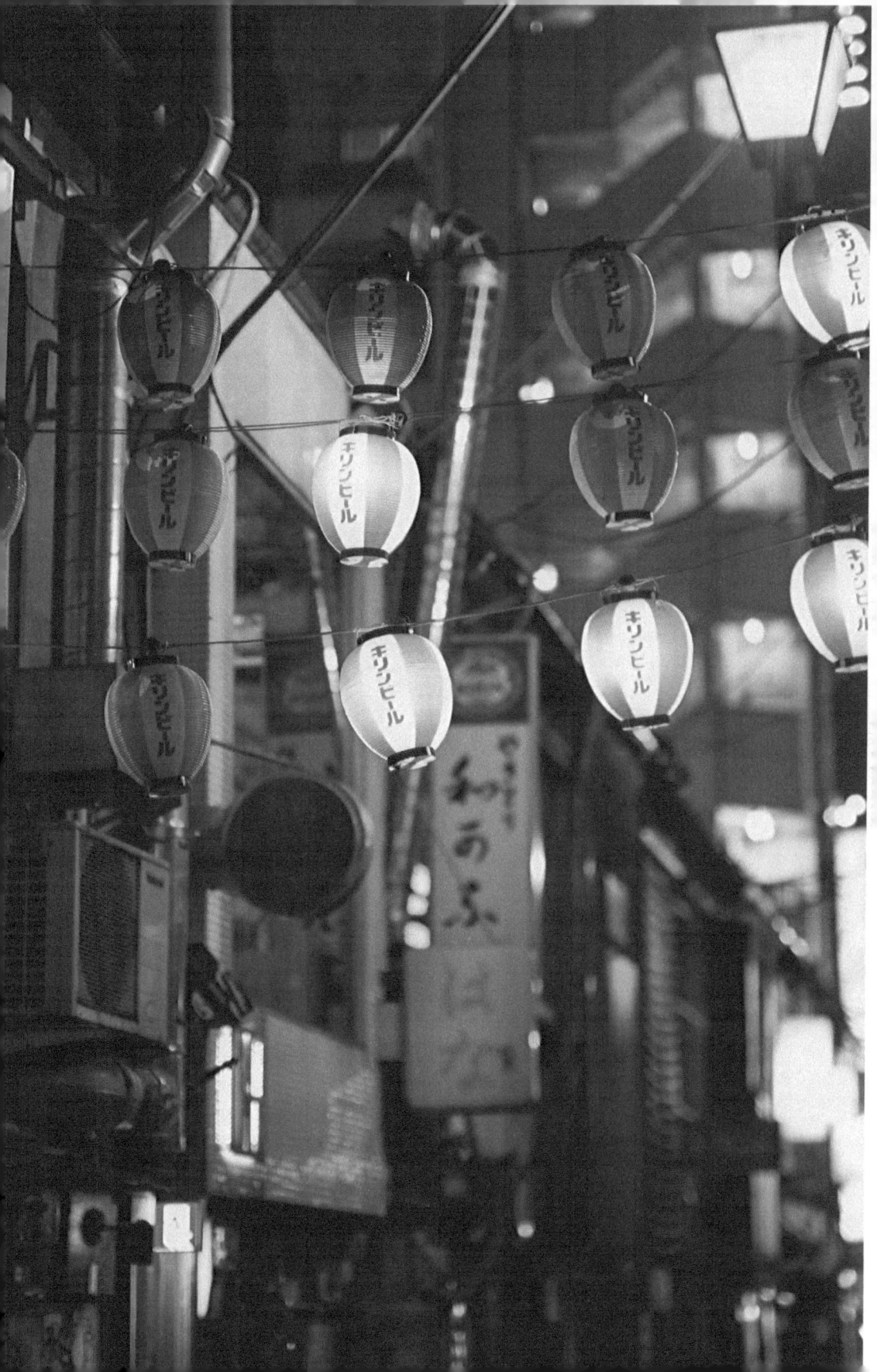

Japan is the most intoxicating place for me. The Japanese culture fascinates me: the food, the dress, the manners and the traditions. It's the travel experience that has moved me the most.
Roman Coppola

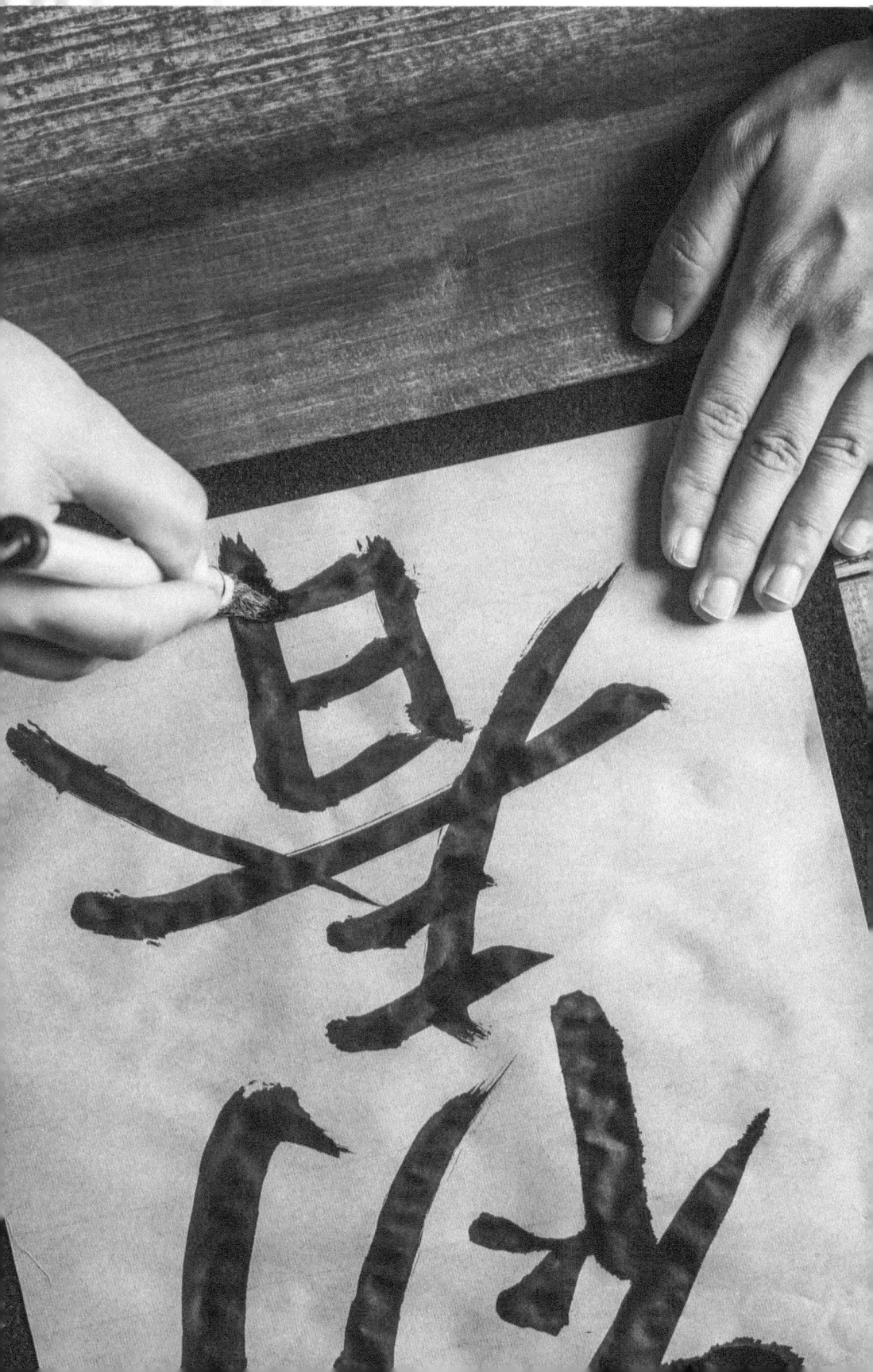

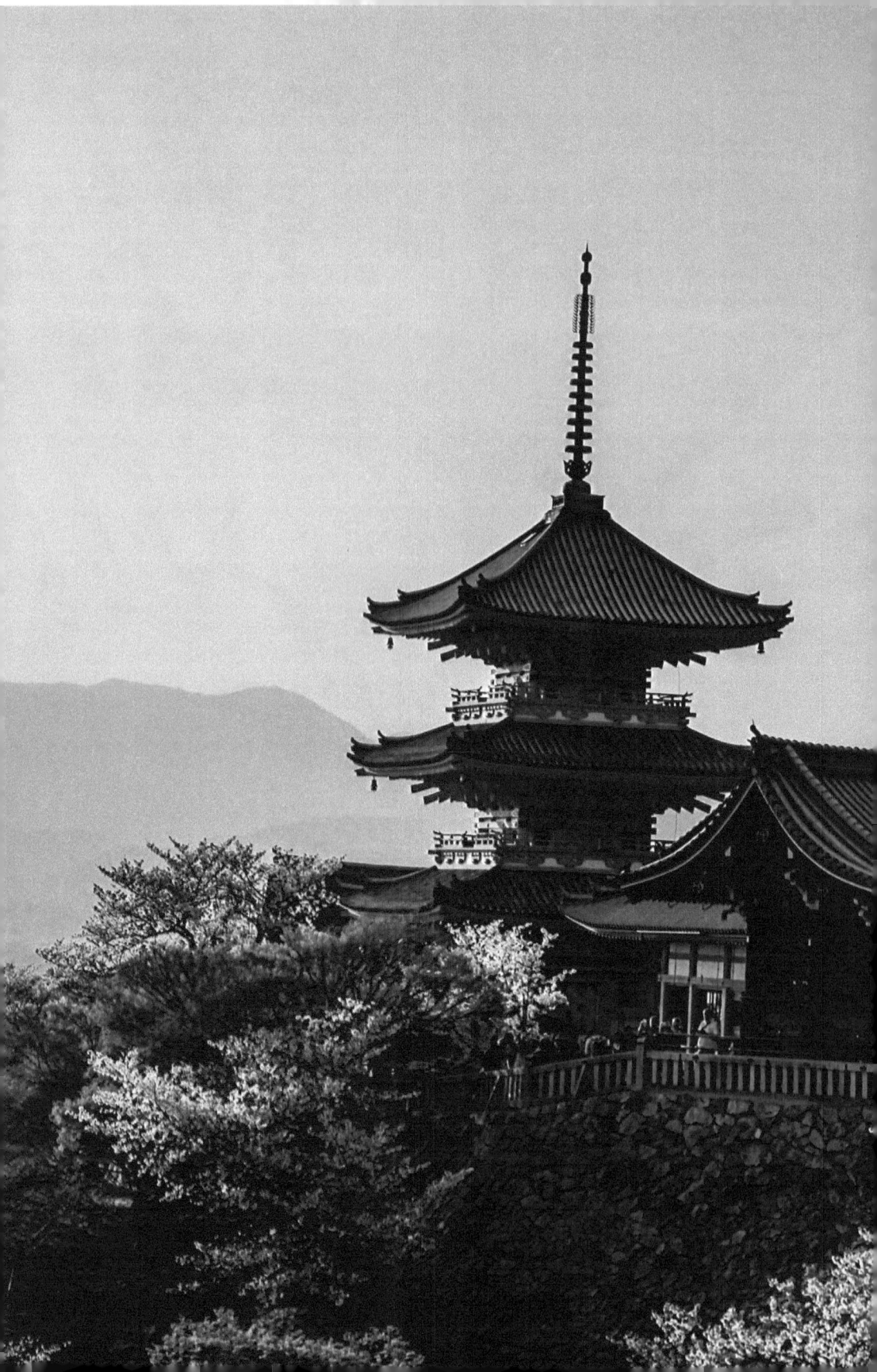

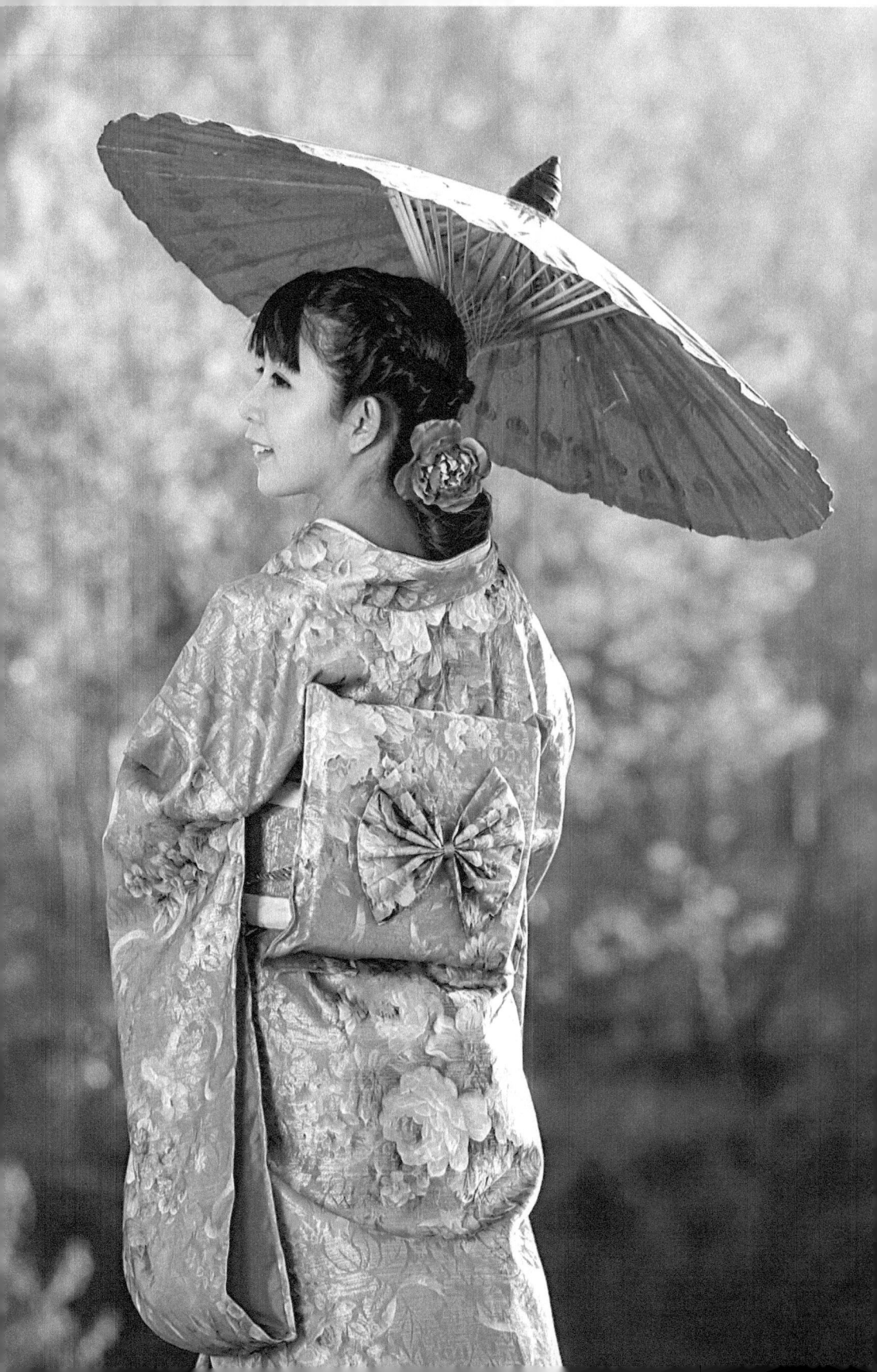

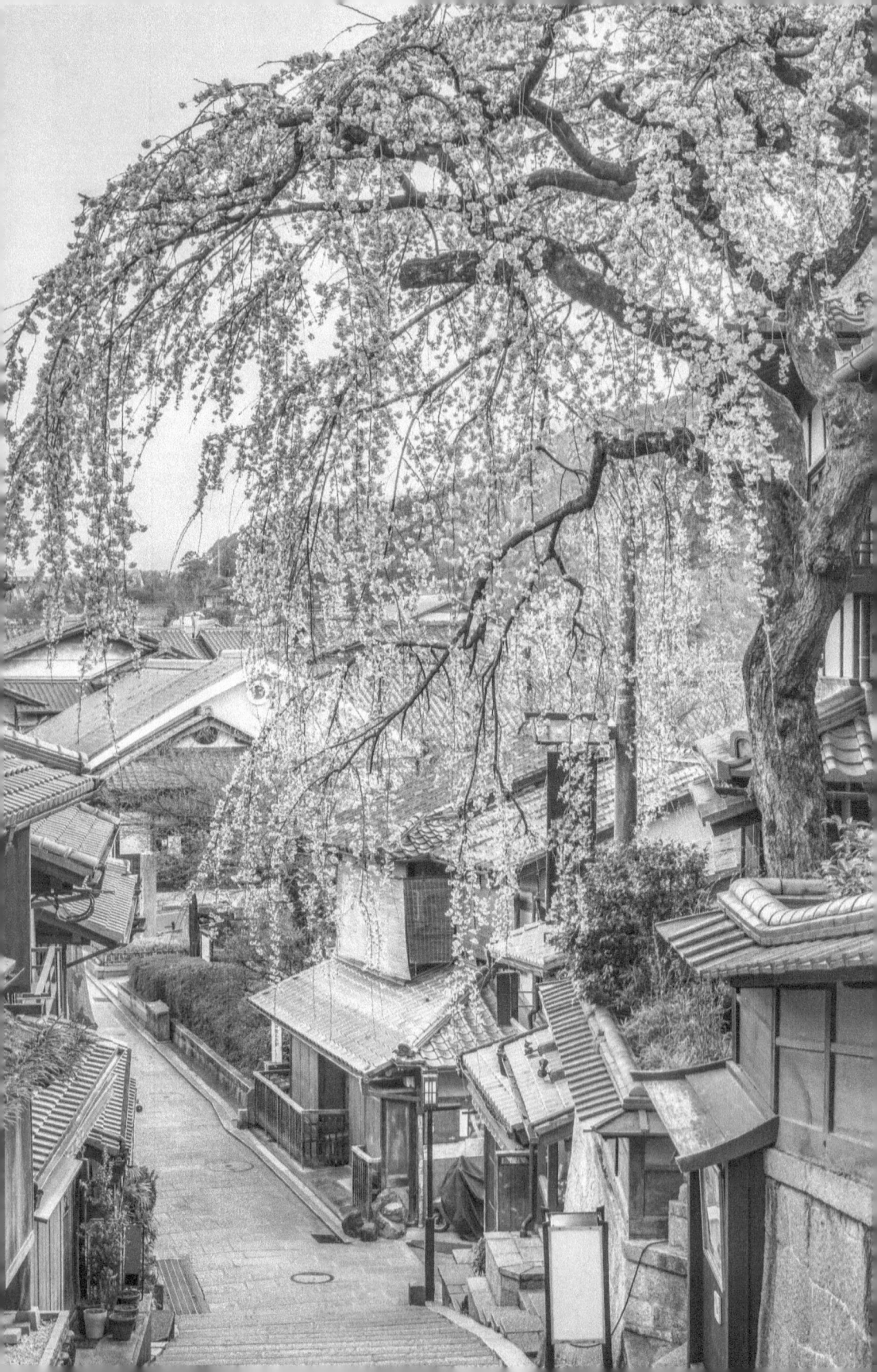

Japan never considers time together as time wasted. Rather, it is time invested.
Donald Richie

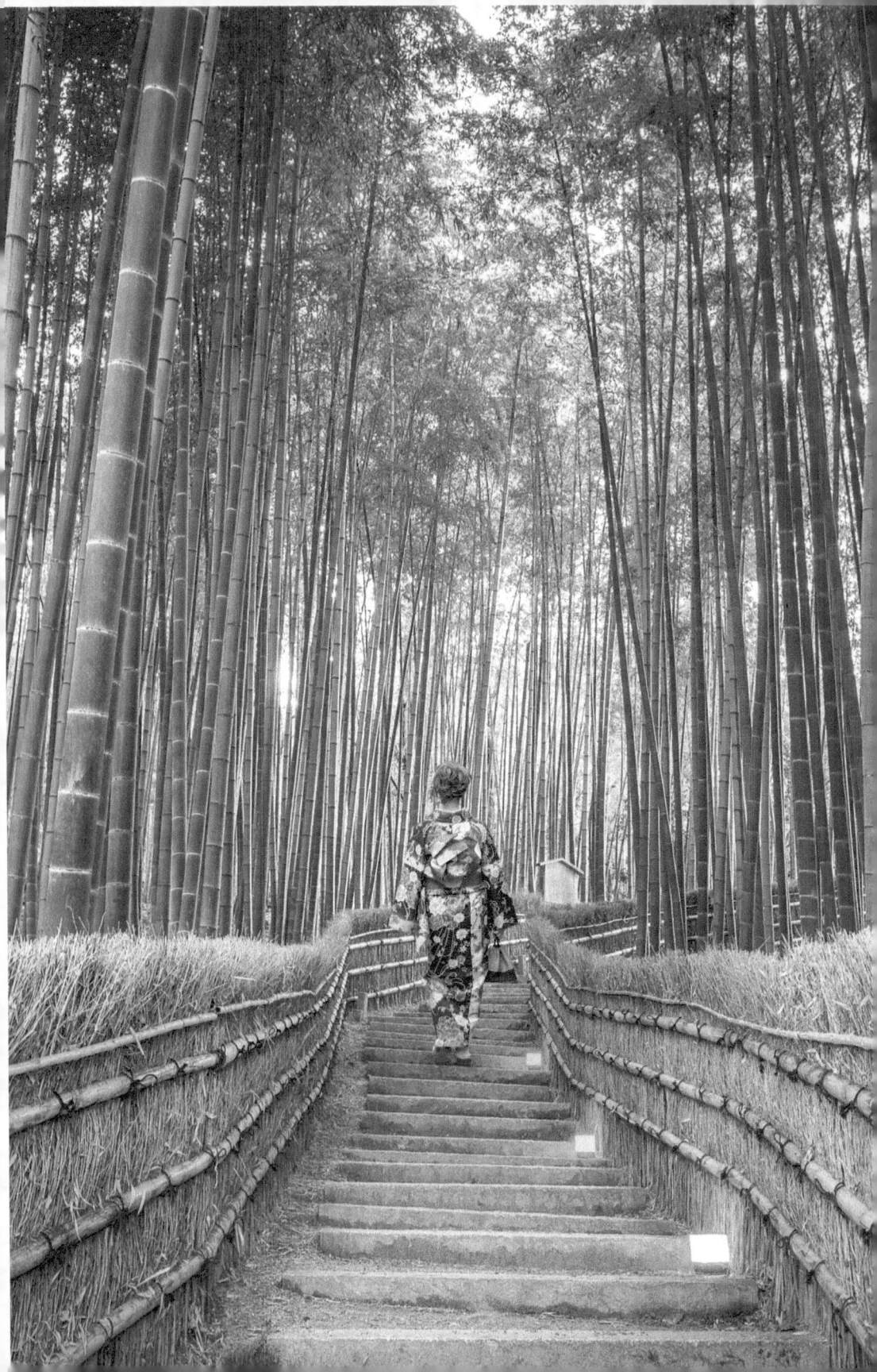

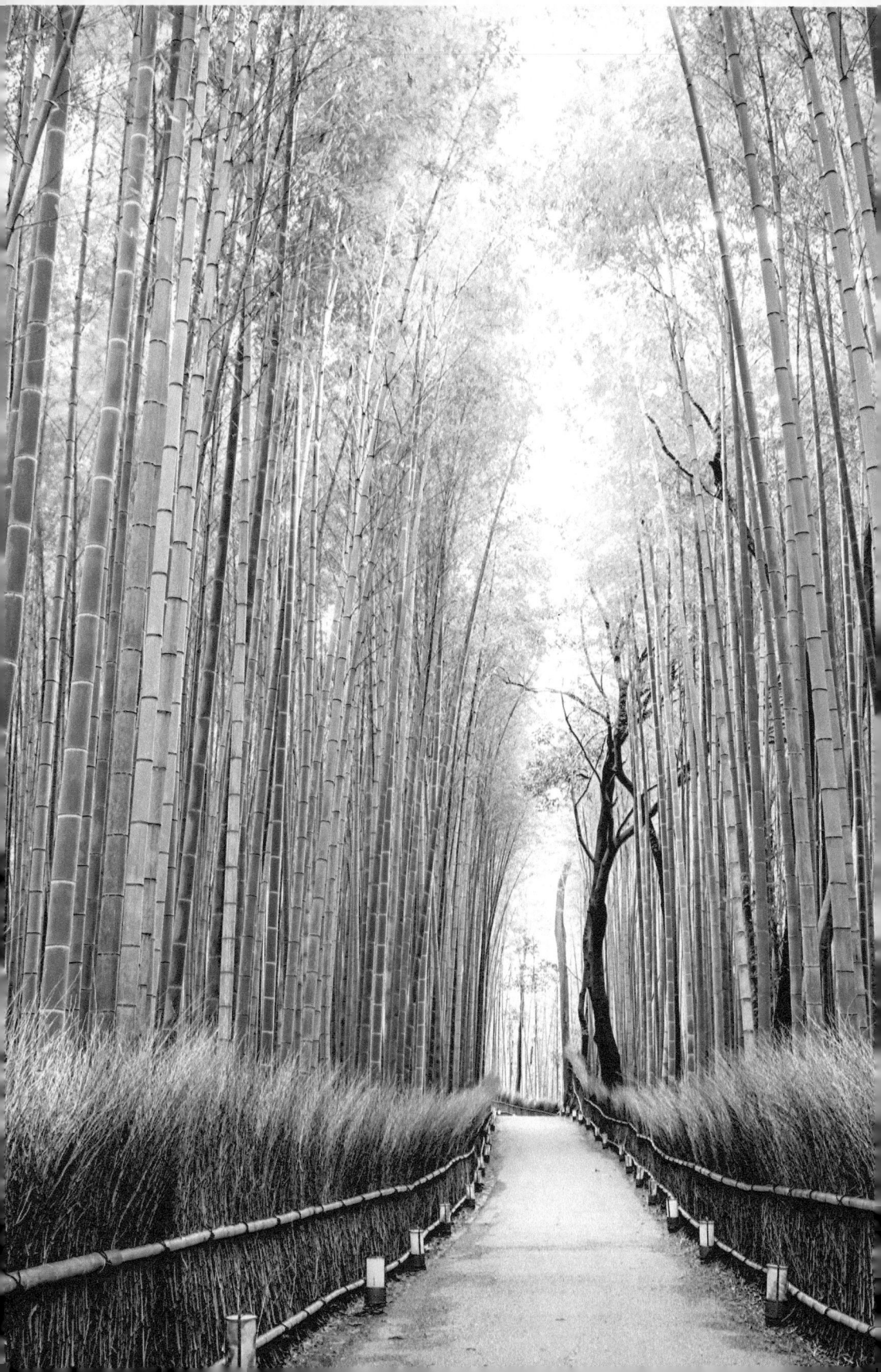

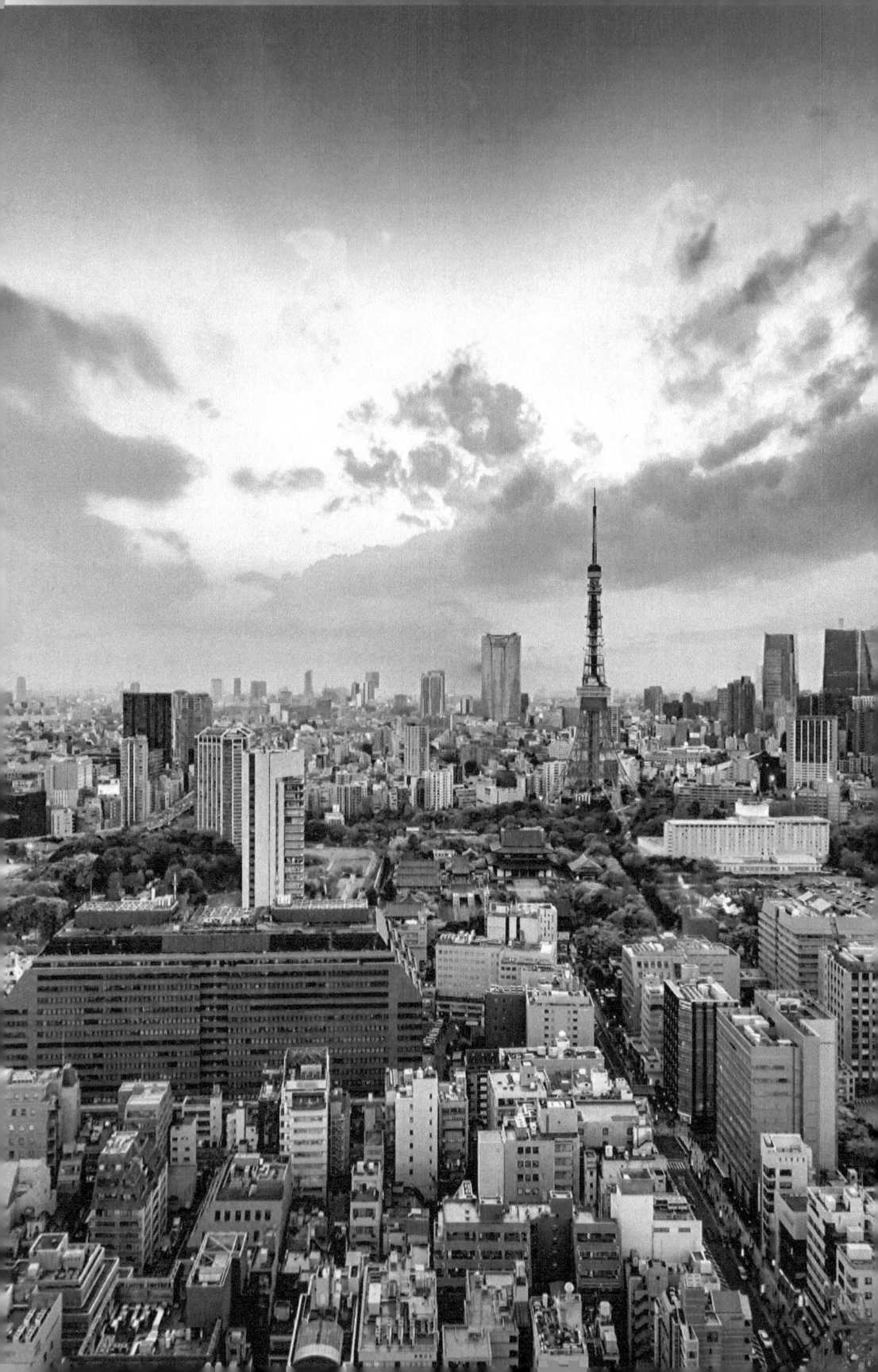

Maitake mushrooms are known in Japan as 'the dancing mushroom.' According to a Japanese legend, a group of Buddhist nuns and woodcutters met on a mountain trail, where they discovered a fruiting of maitake mushrooms emerging from the forest floor. Rejoicing at their discovery of this delicious mushroom, they danced to celebrate.

Paul Stamets

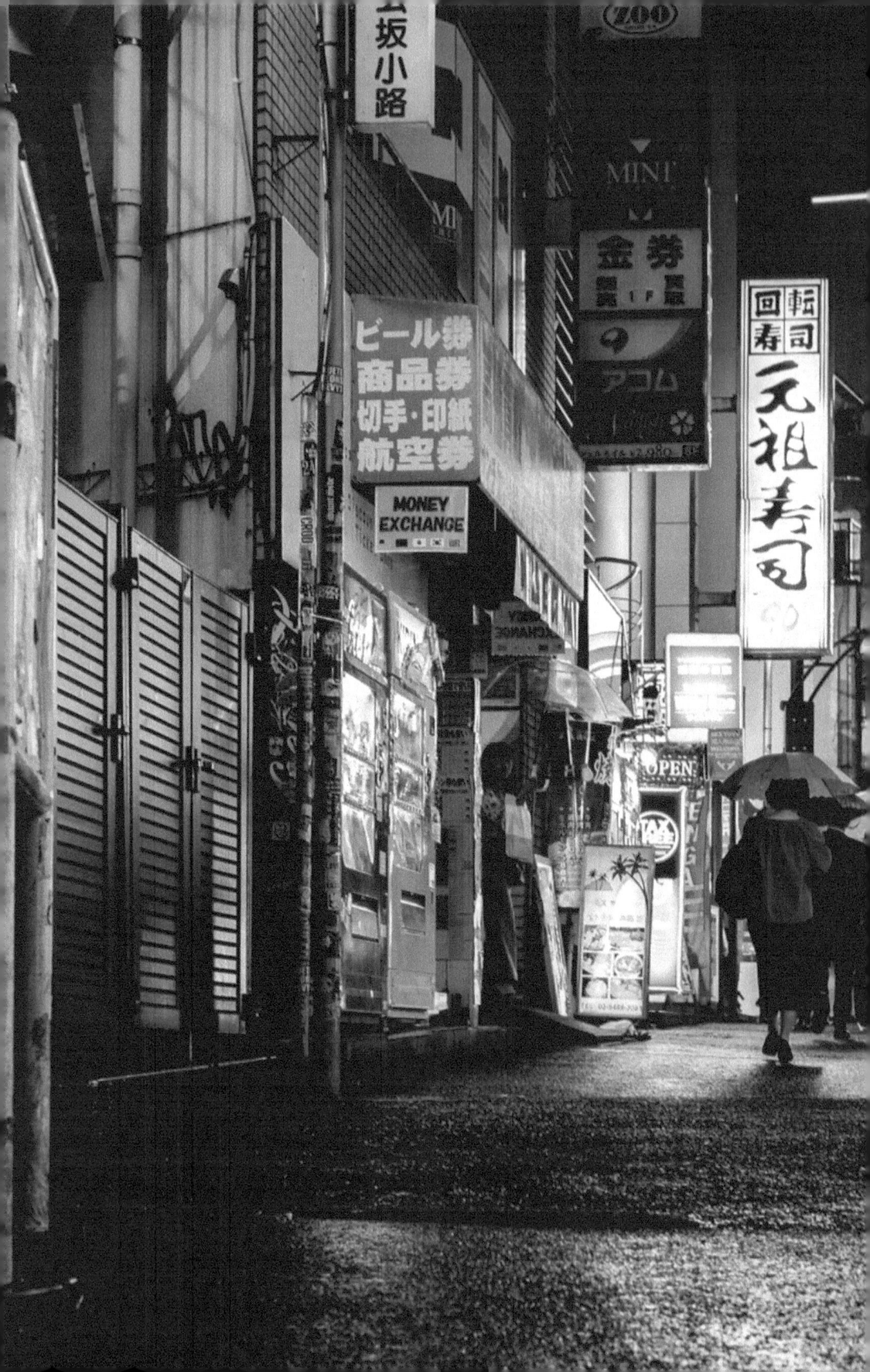

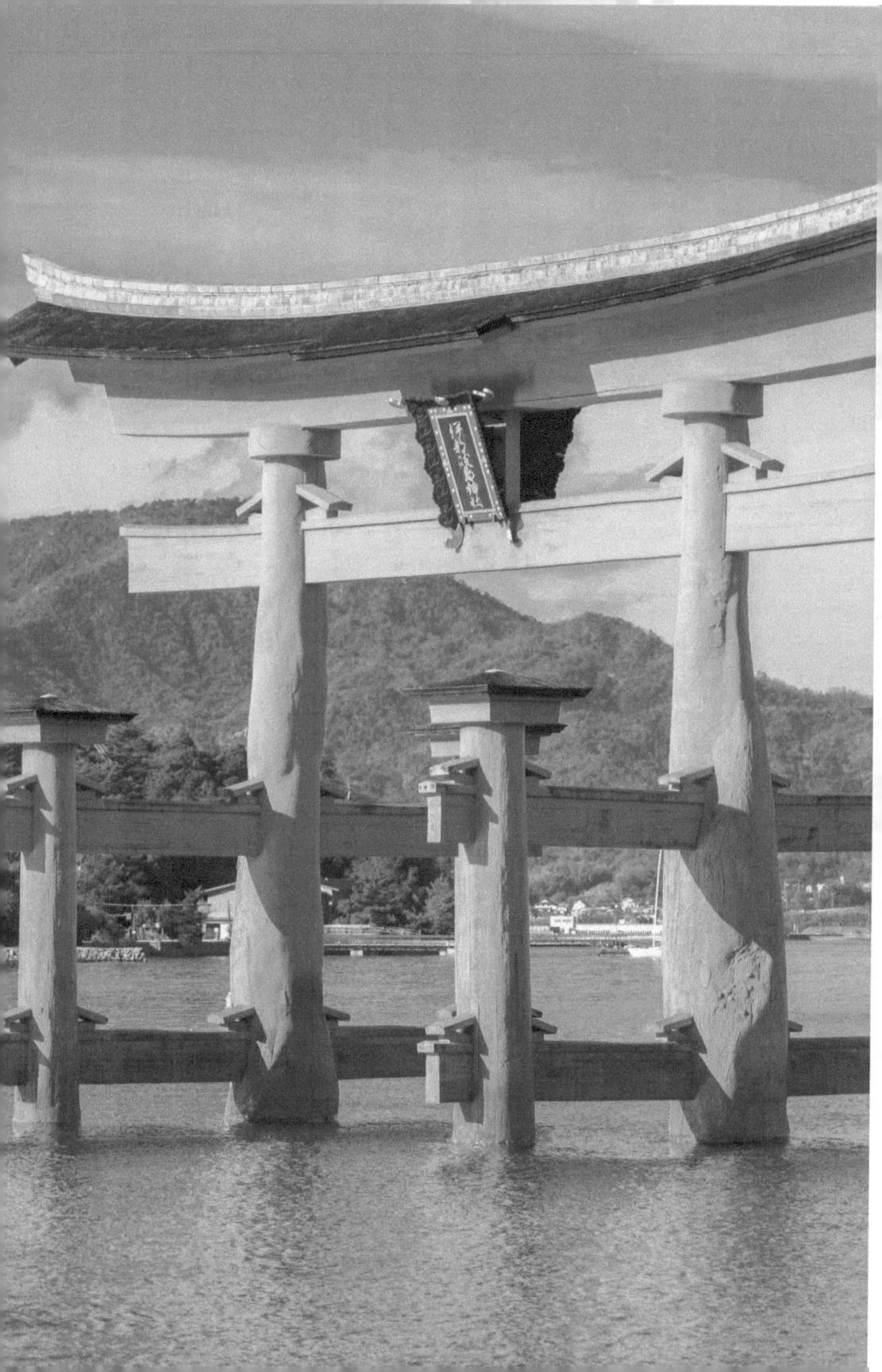

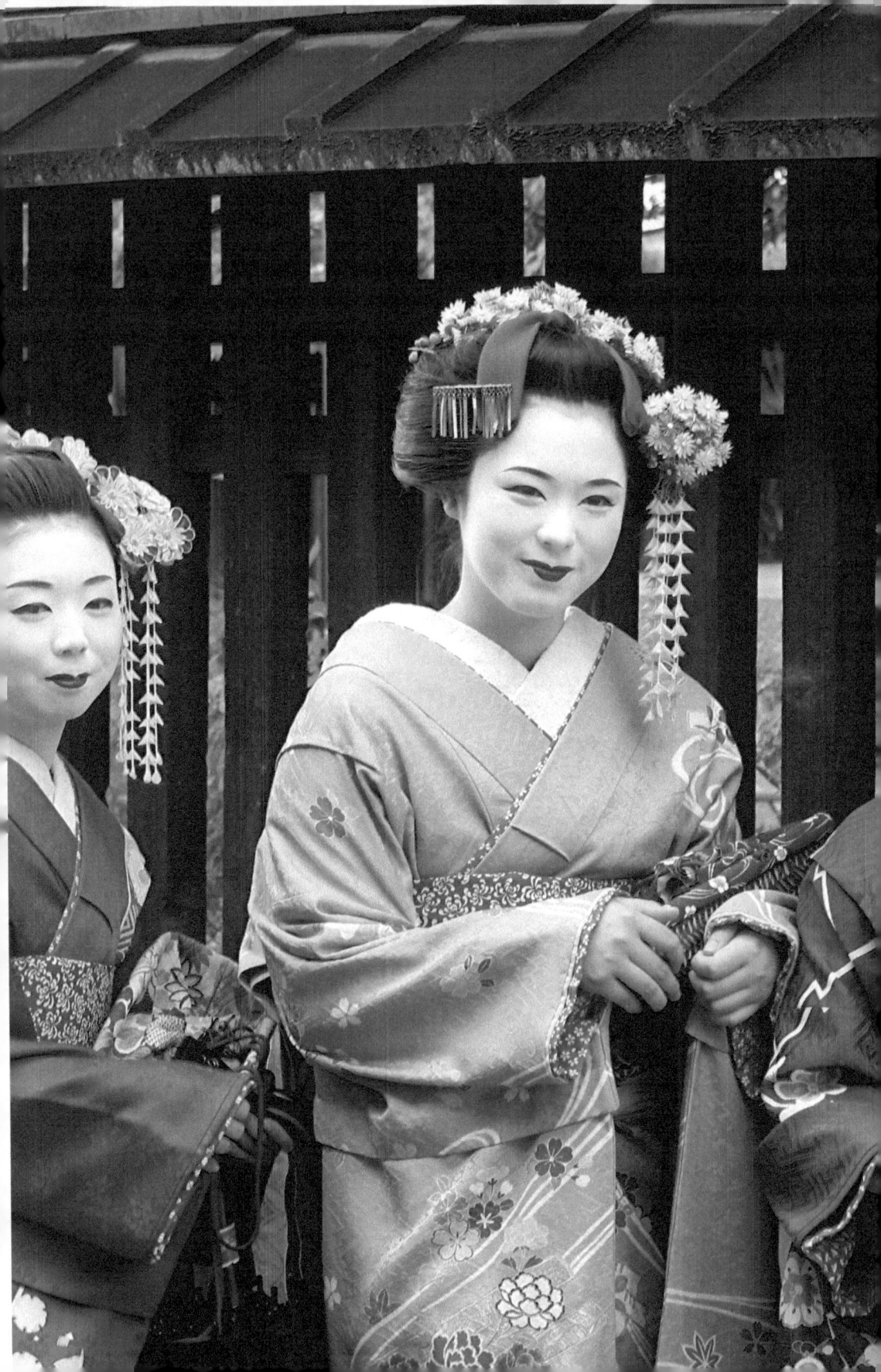

Teaism is a cult founded on the adoration of the beautiful among the sordid facts of everyday existence.
Kakuzo Okahura

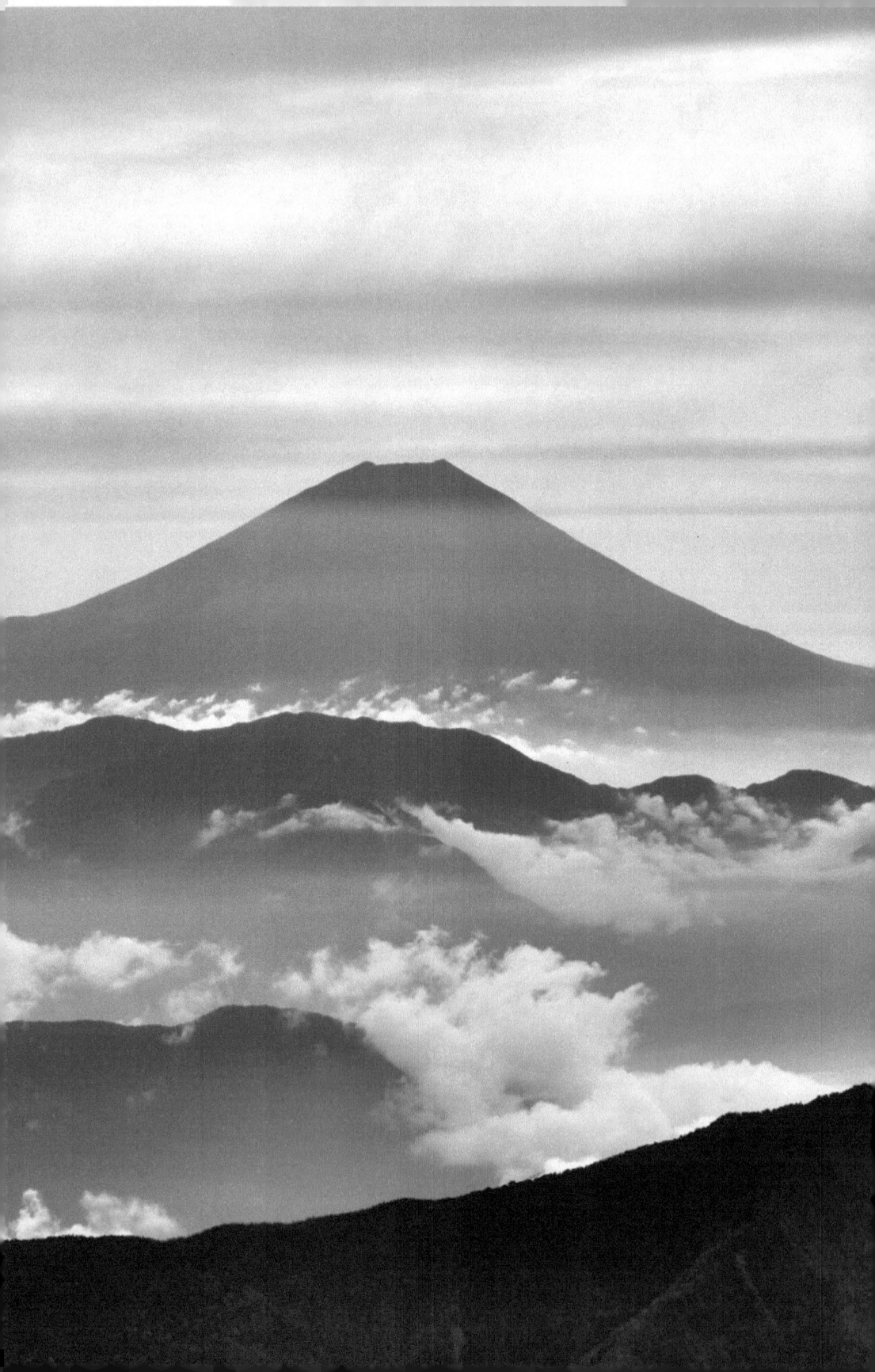

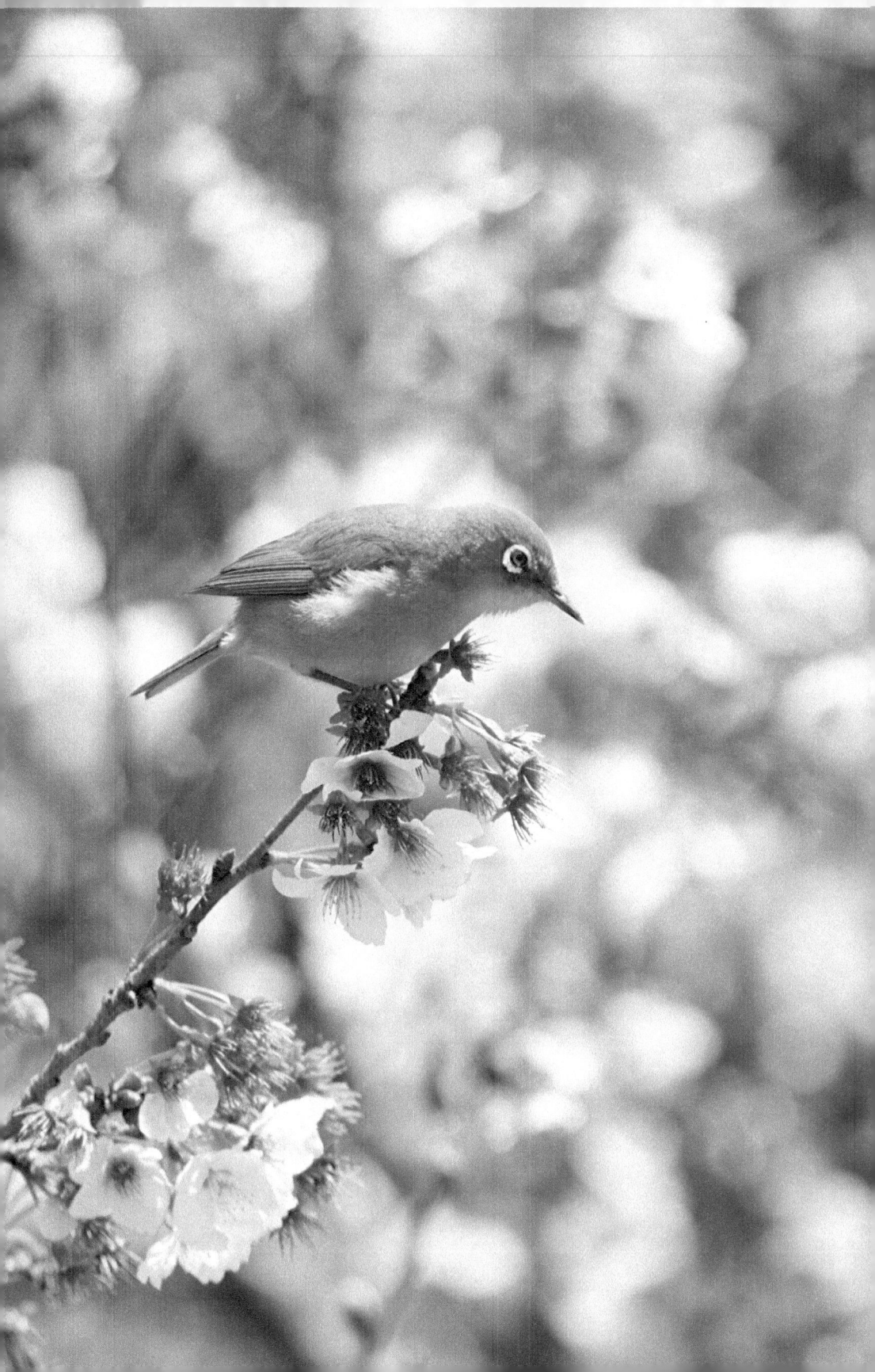

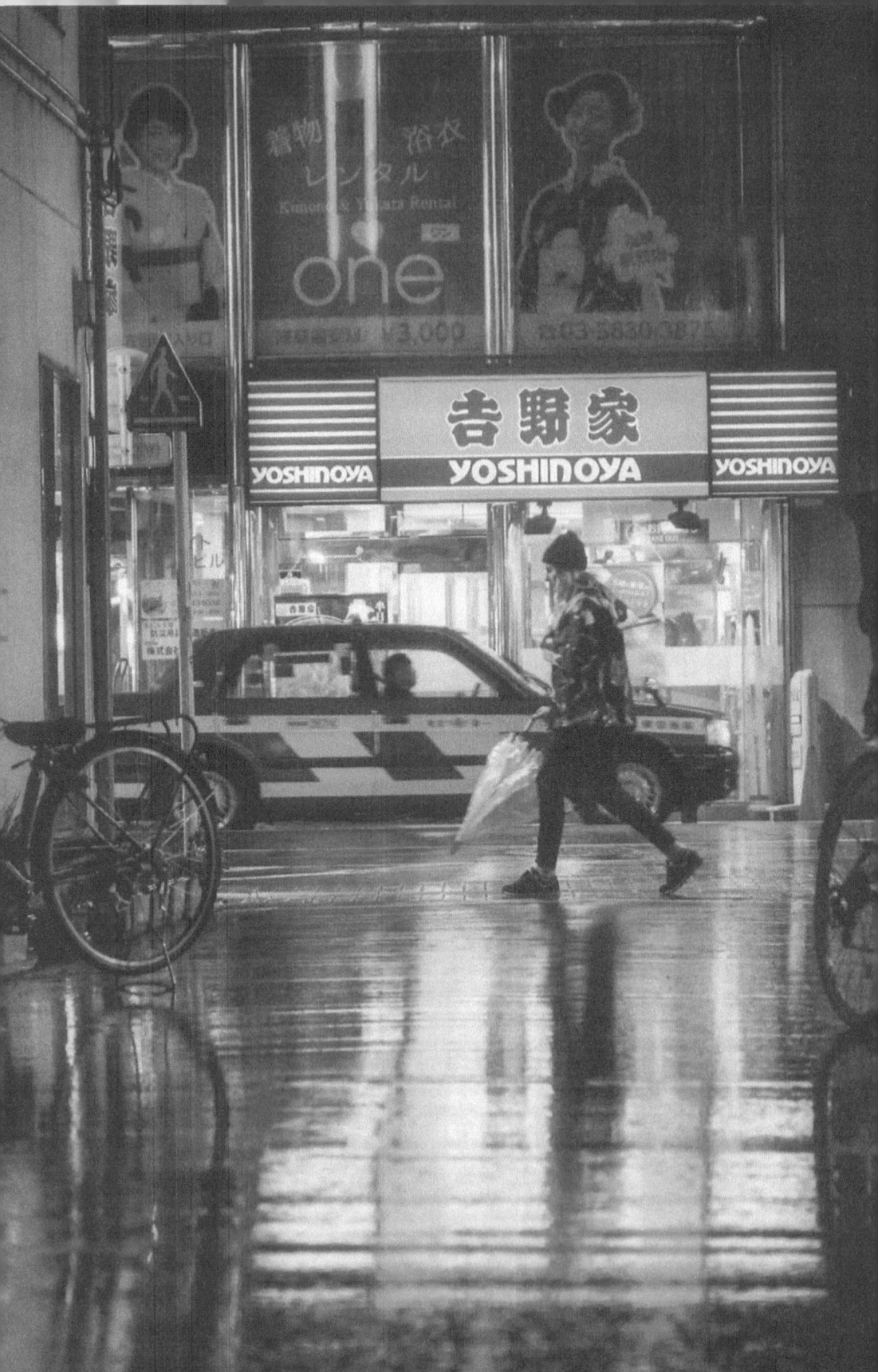

One glass of water doesn't equal another. One may just appease the thirst, the other you may enjoy thoroughly. In Japan, people know about this difference.
Jil Sander

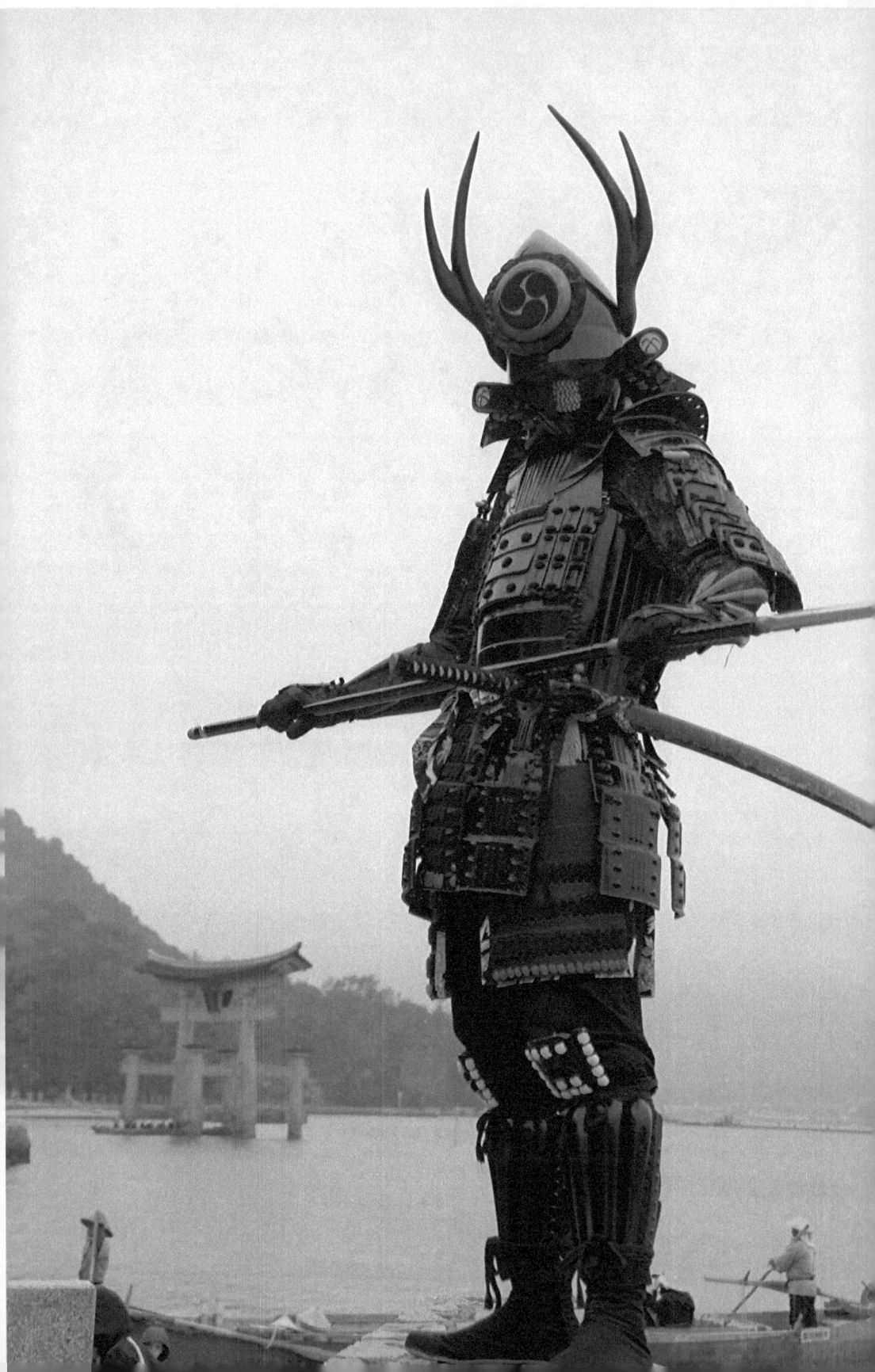

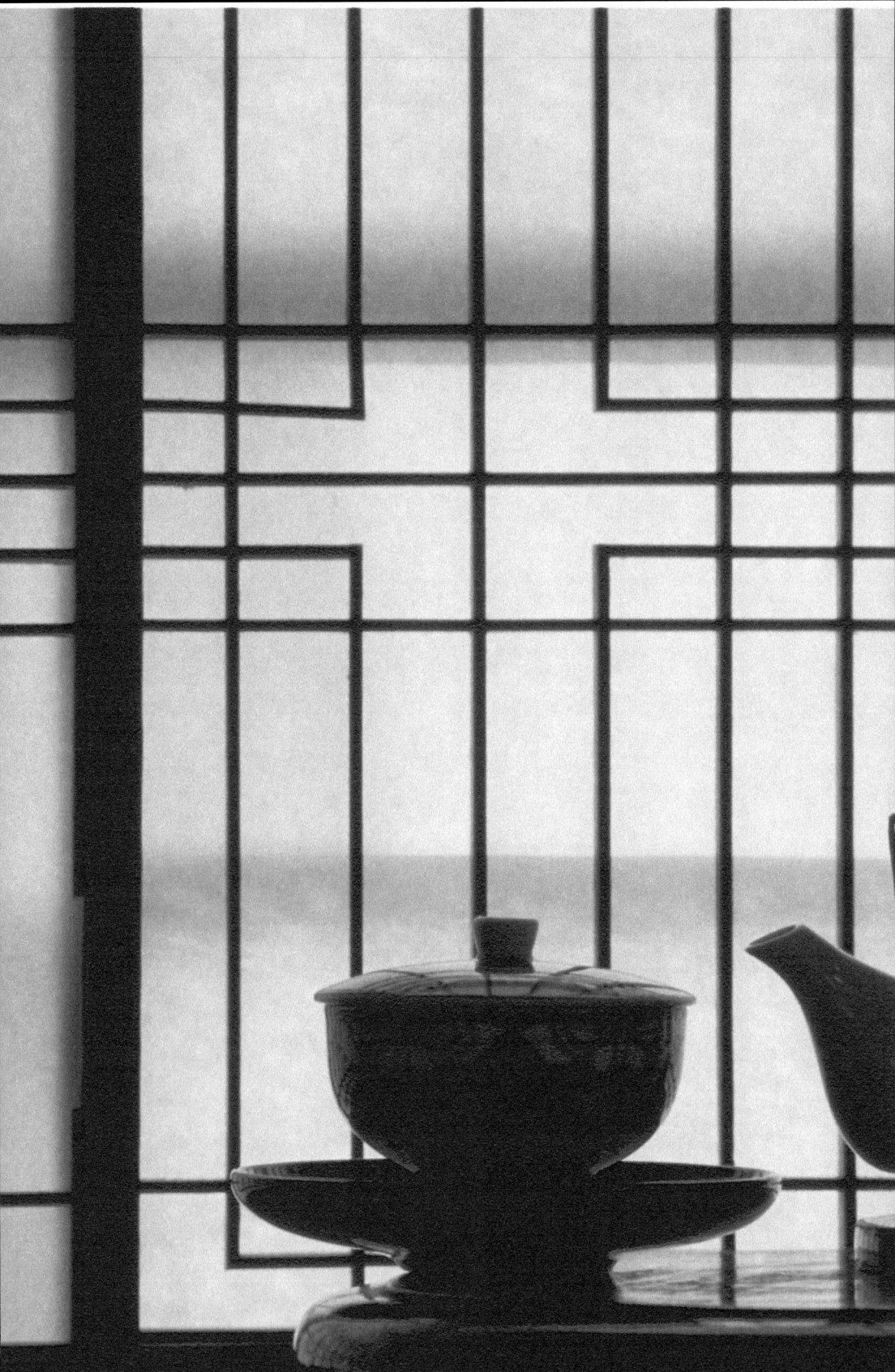

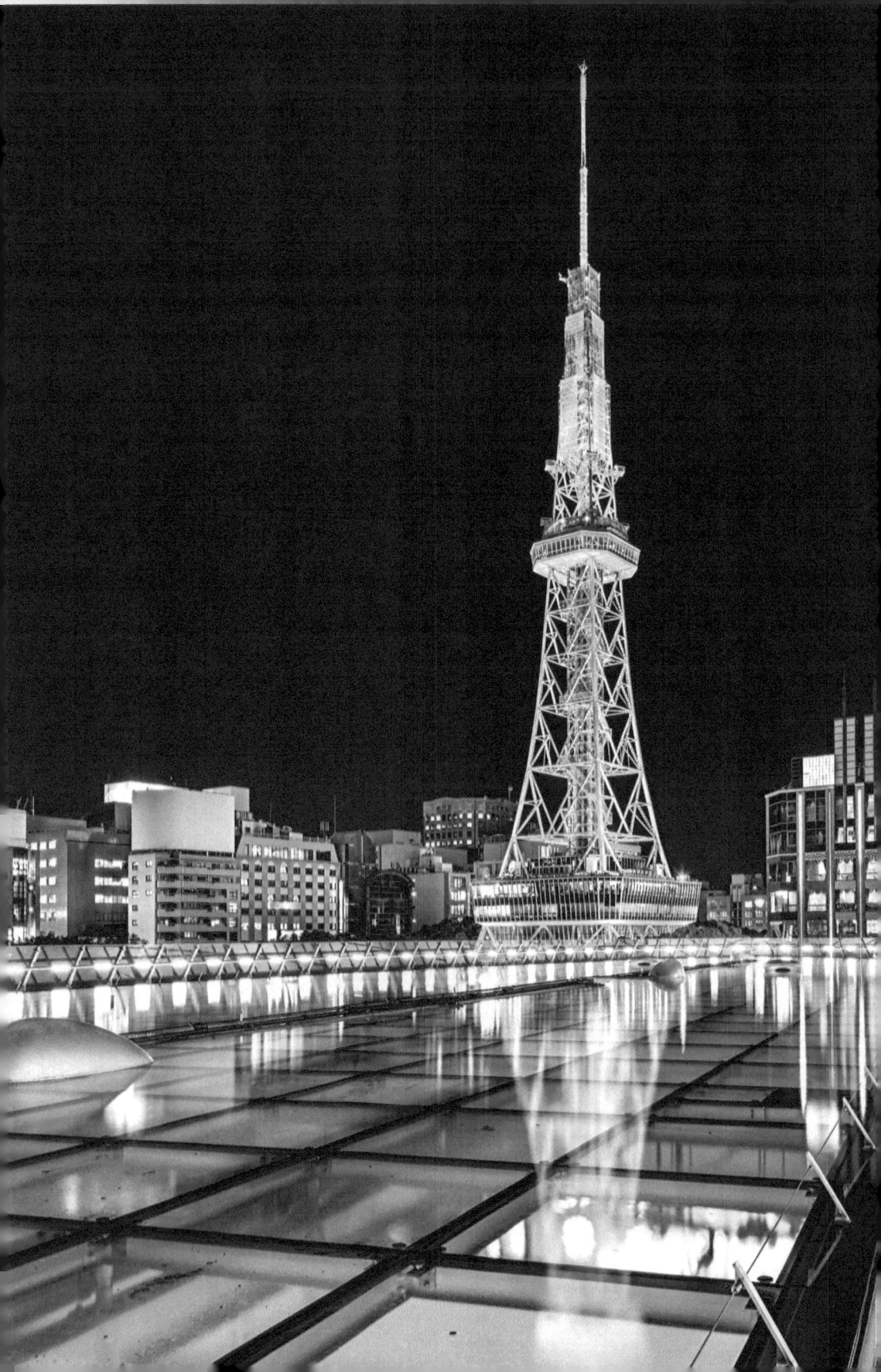

What they have done in Japan, which I find so inspirational, is they've brought the toilet out from behind the locked door. They've made it conversational. People go out and upgrade their toilet. They talk about it. They've sanitized it.
Rose George

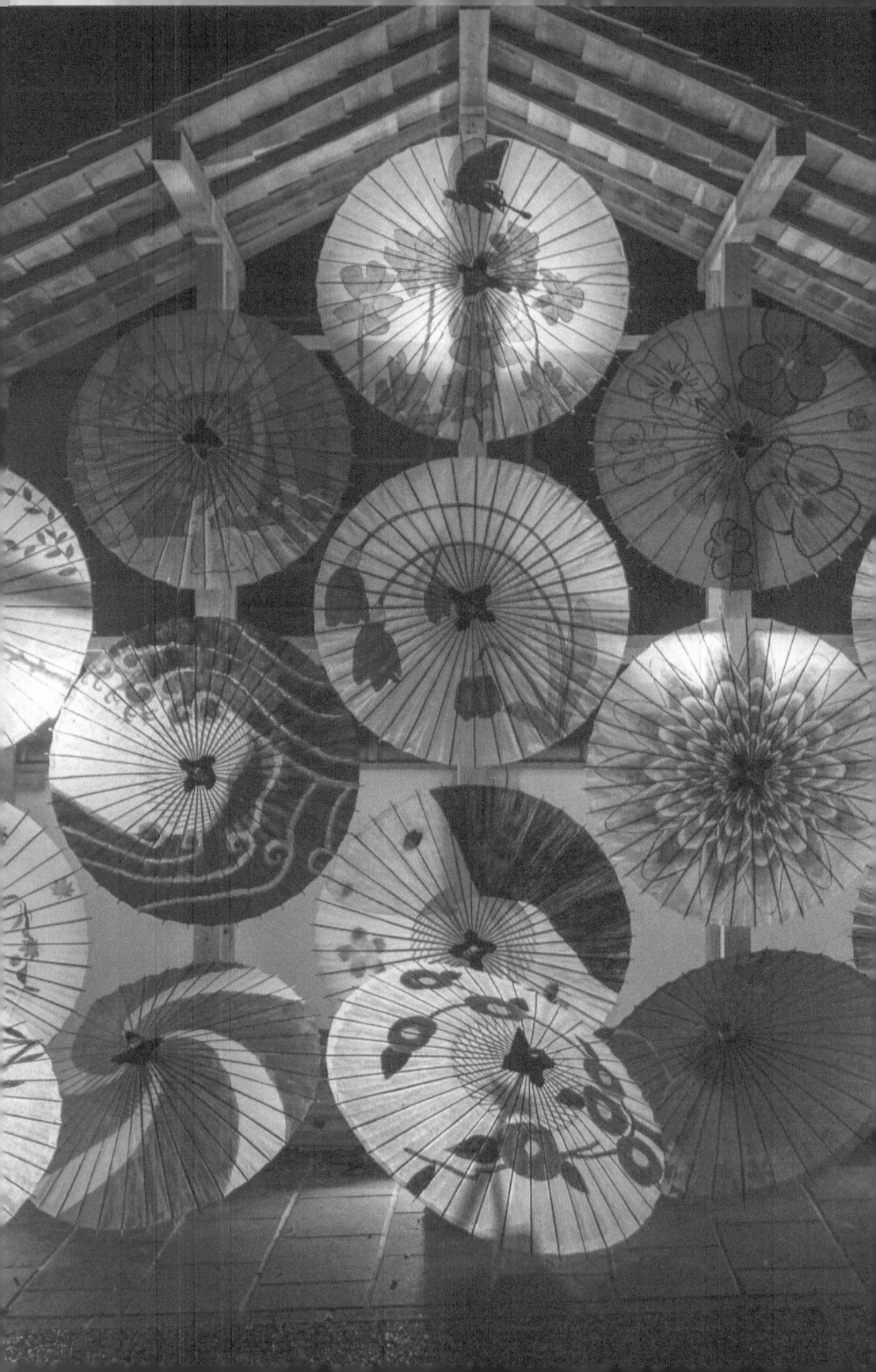

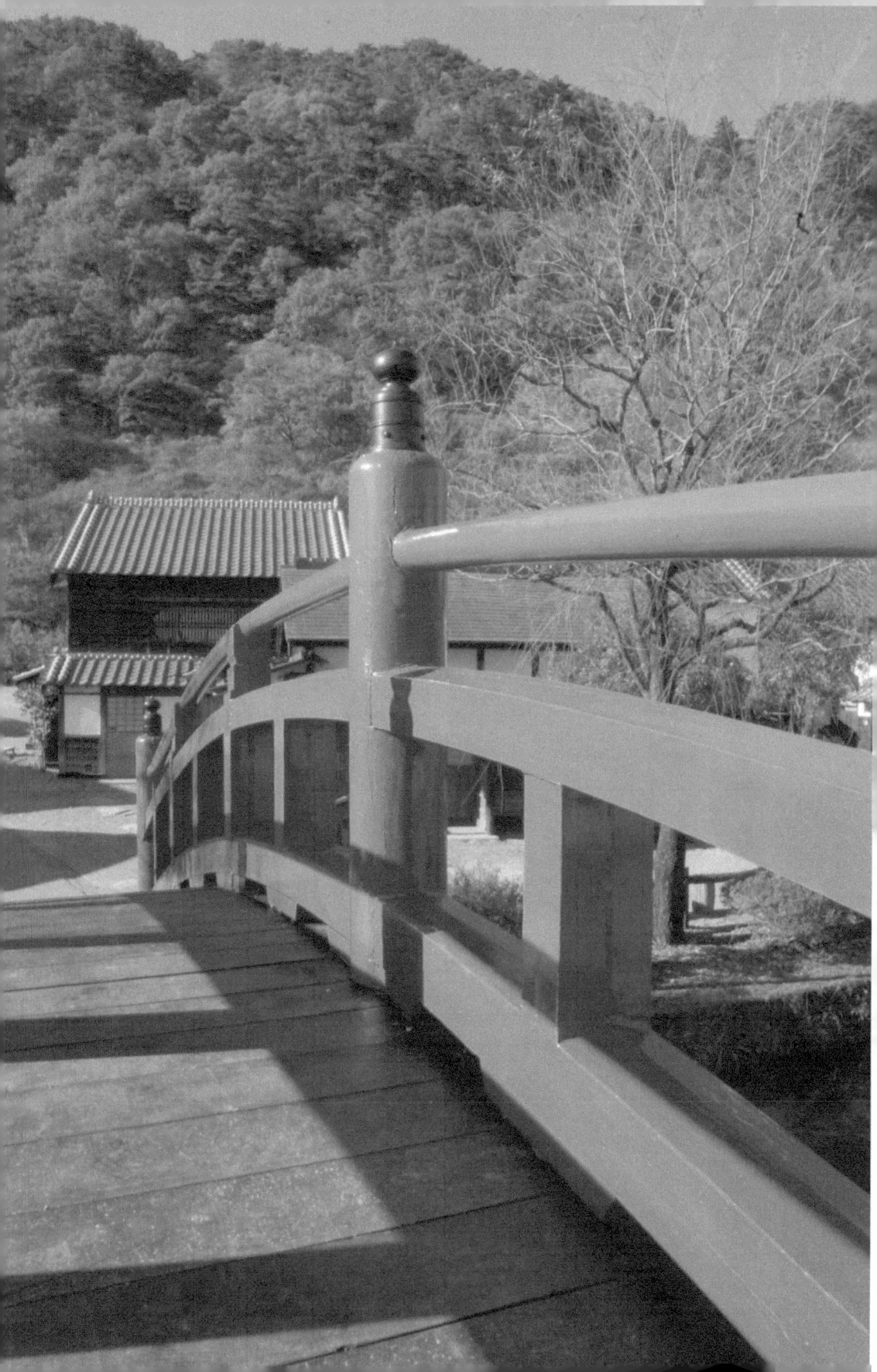

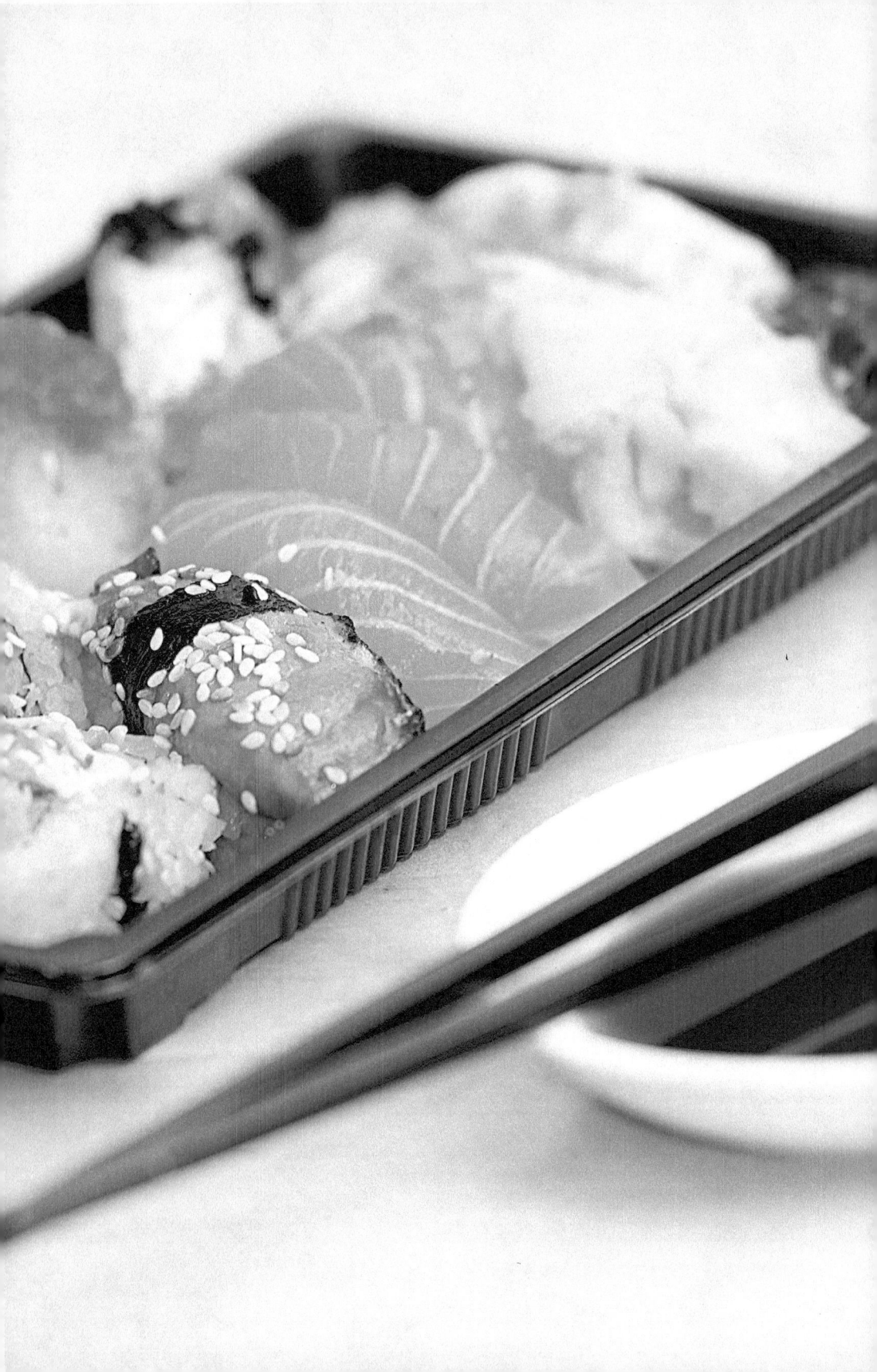

Japan is very cosmopolitan – it values its origins, but a world view hovers above this narrow perspective. The interest of the Japanese in their folk culture is transcendental.
F. Sionil Jose

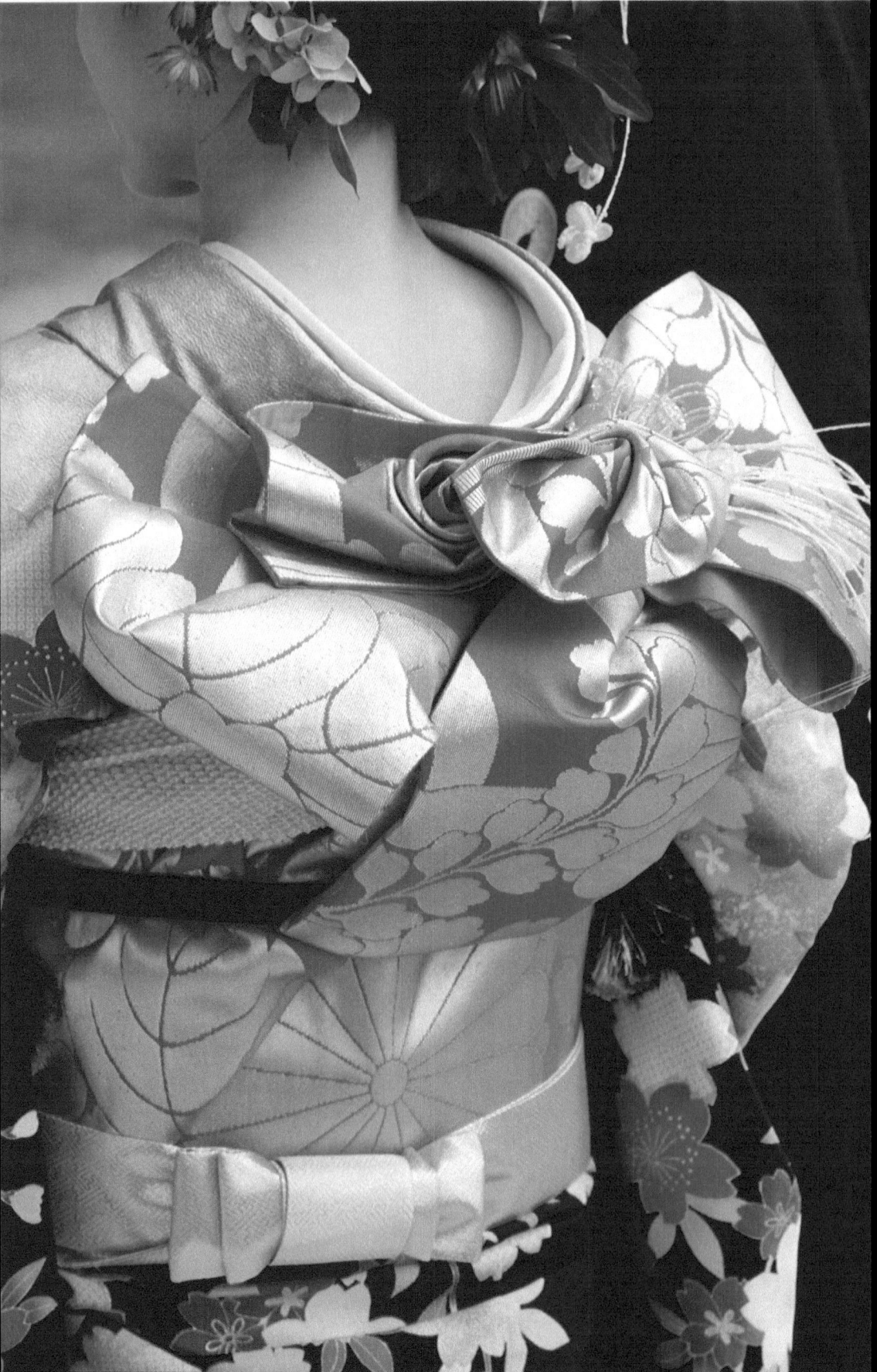

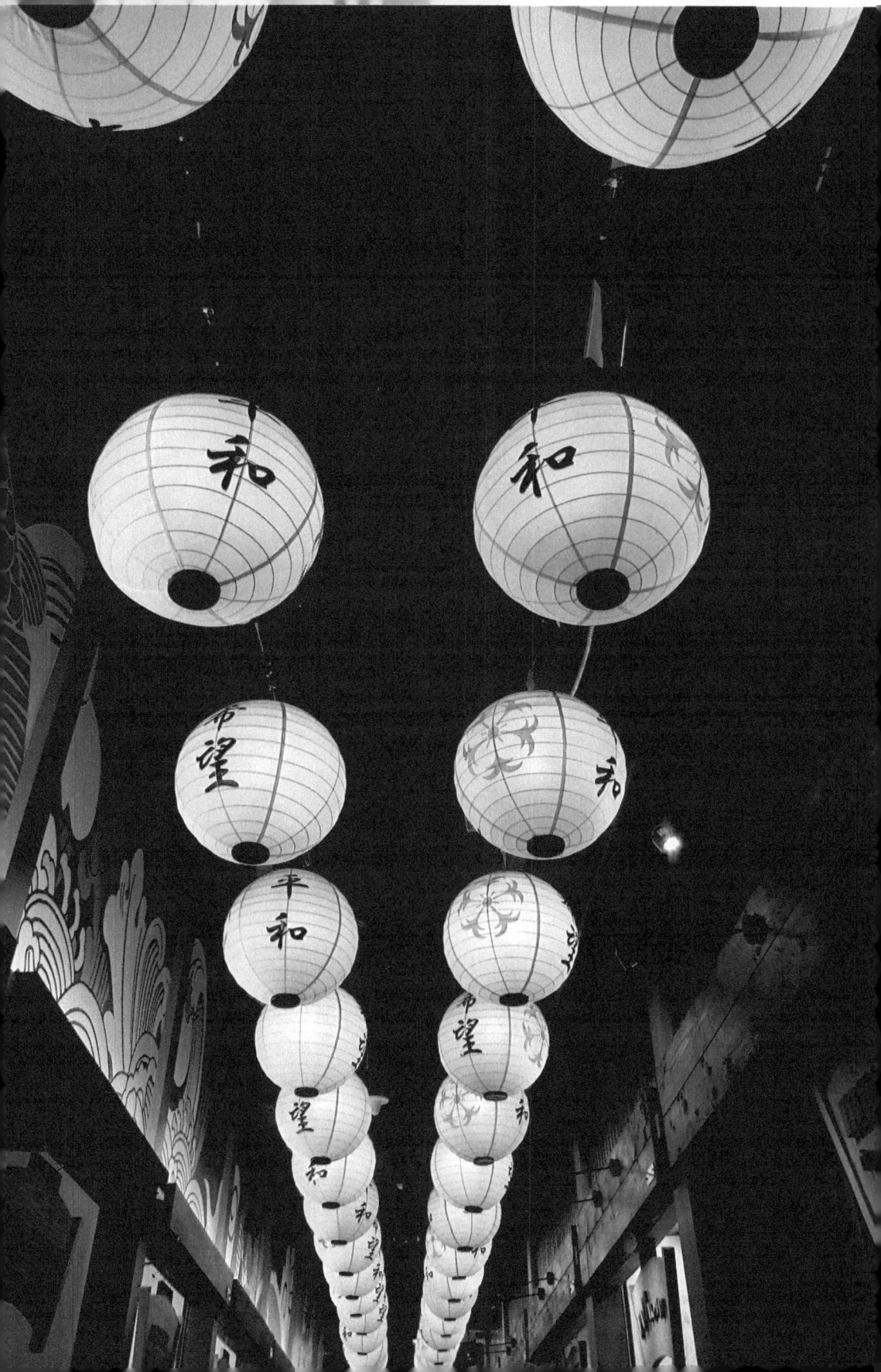

If your computer speaks English, it was probably made in Japan.
Alan Perlis

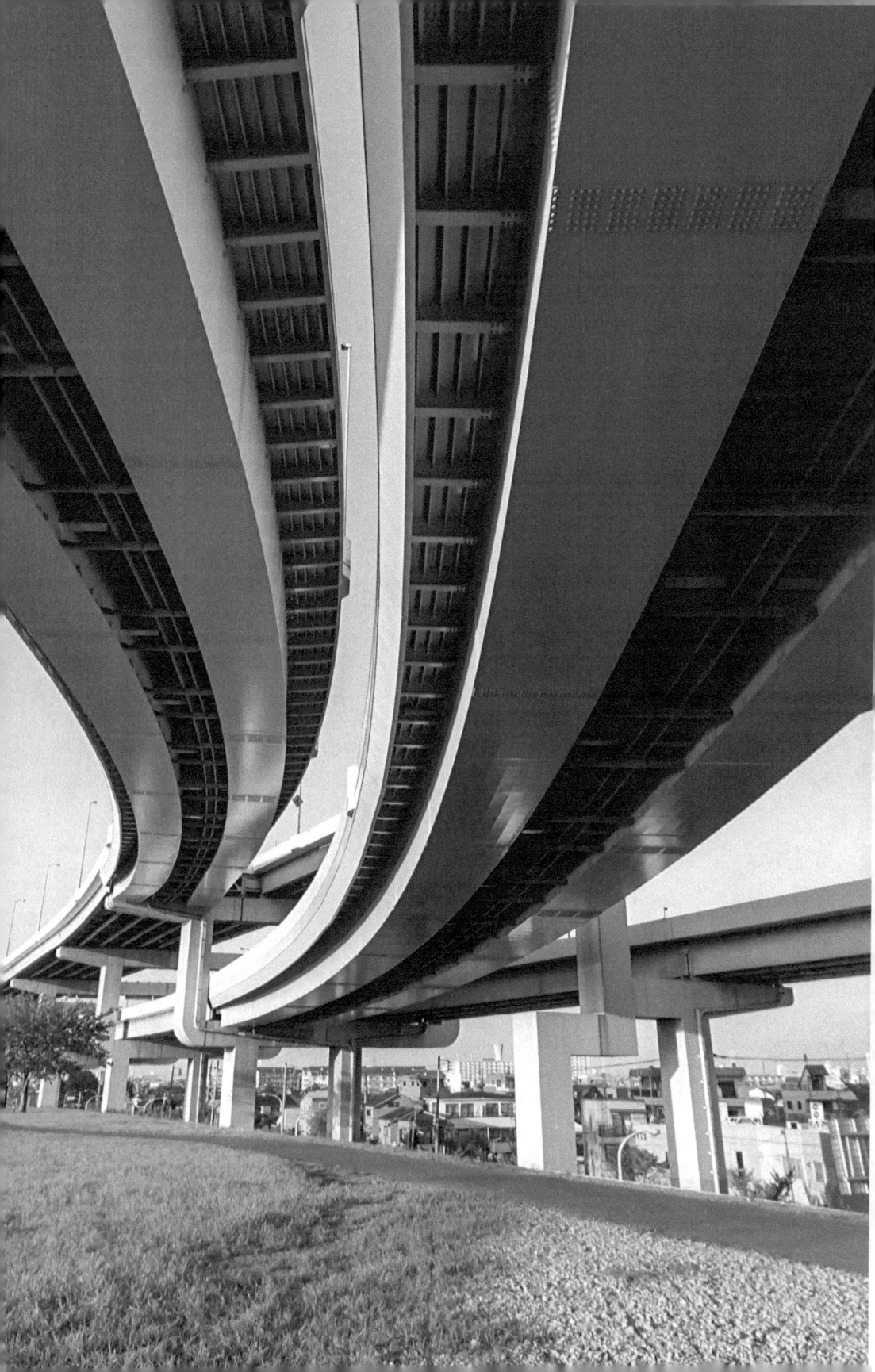

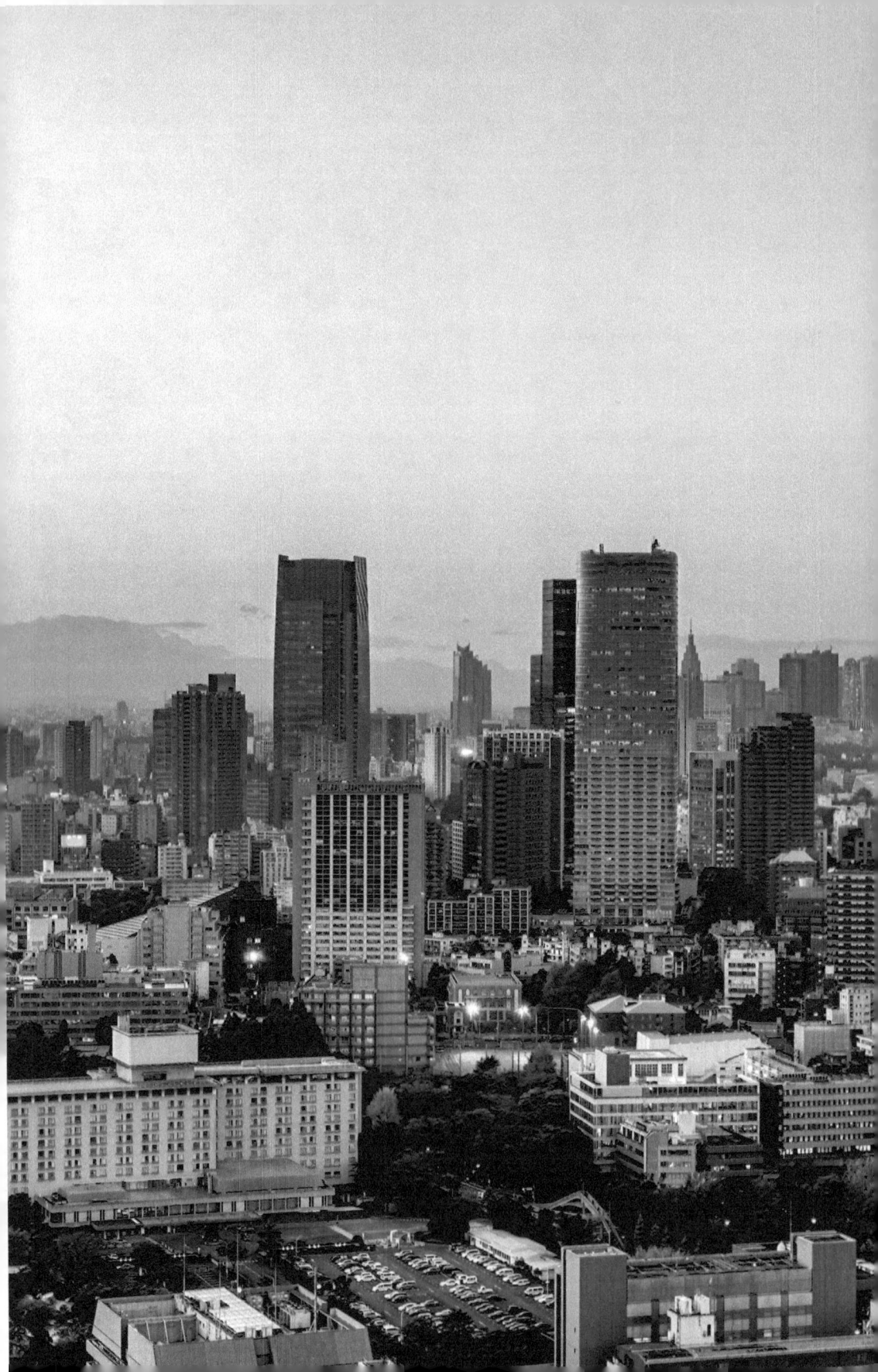

Japan, not only a mega-busy city that thrives on electronics and efficiency, actually has an almost sacred appreciation of nature. One must travel outside of Tokyo to truly experience the 'old Japan' and more importantly feel these aspects of Japanese culture.
Apolo Ohno

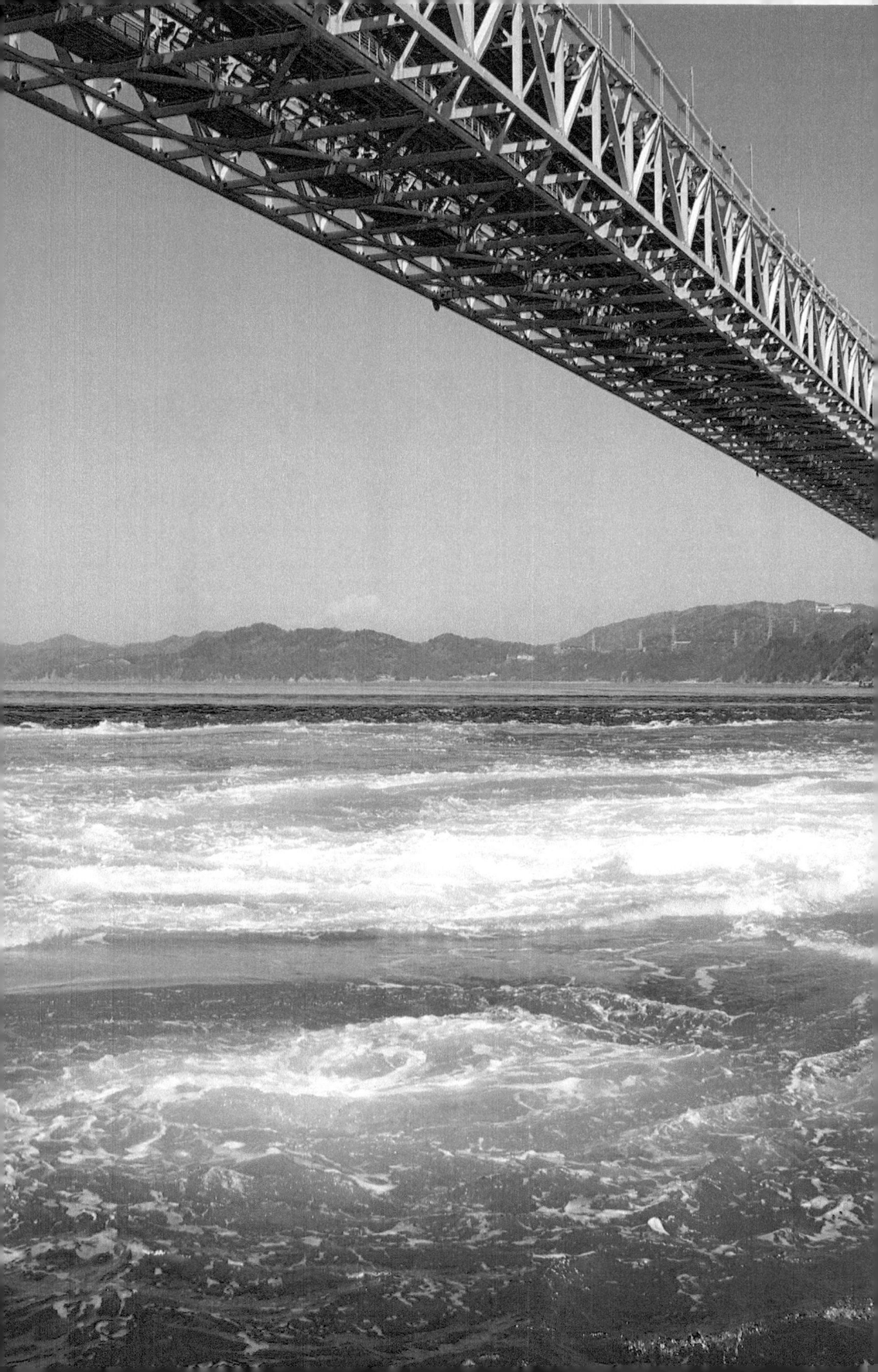

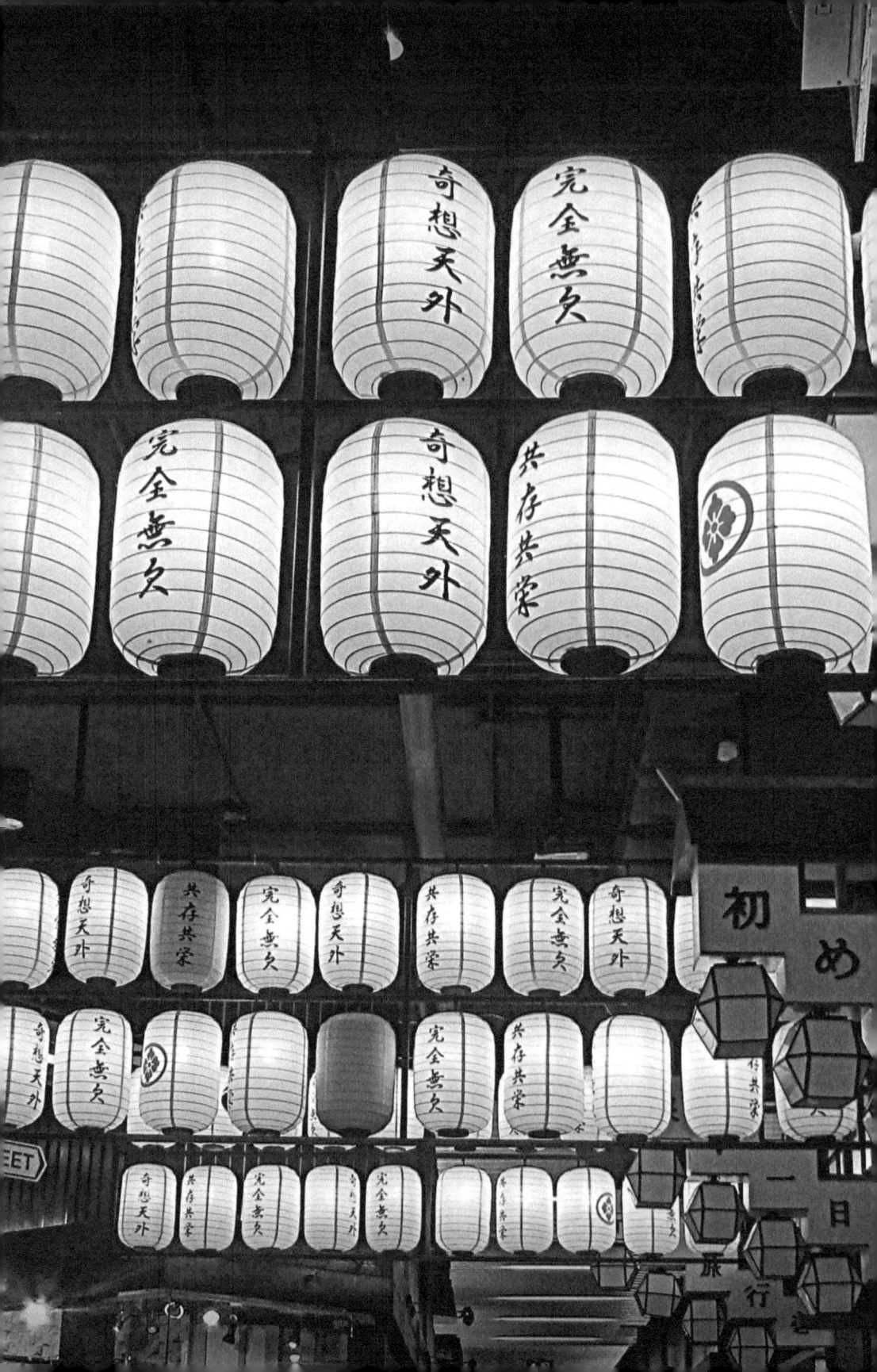

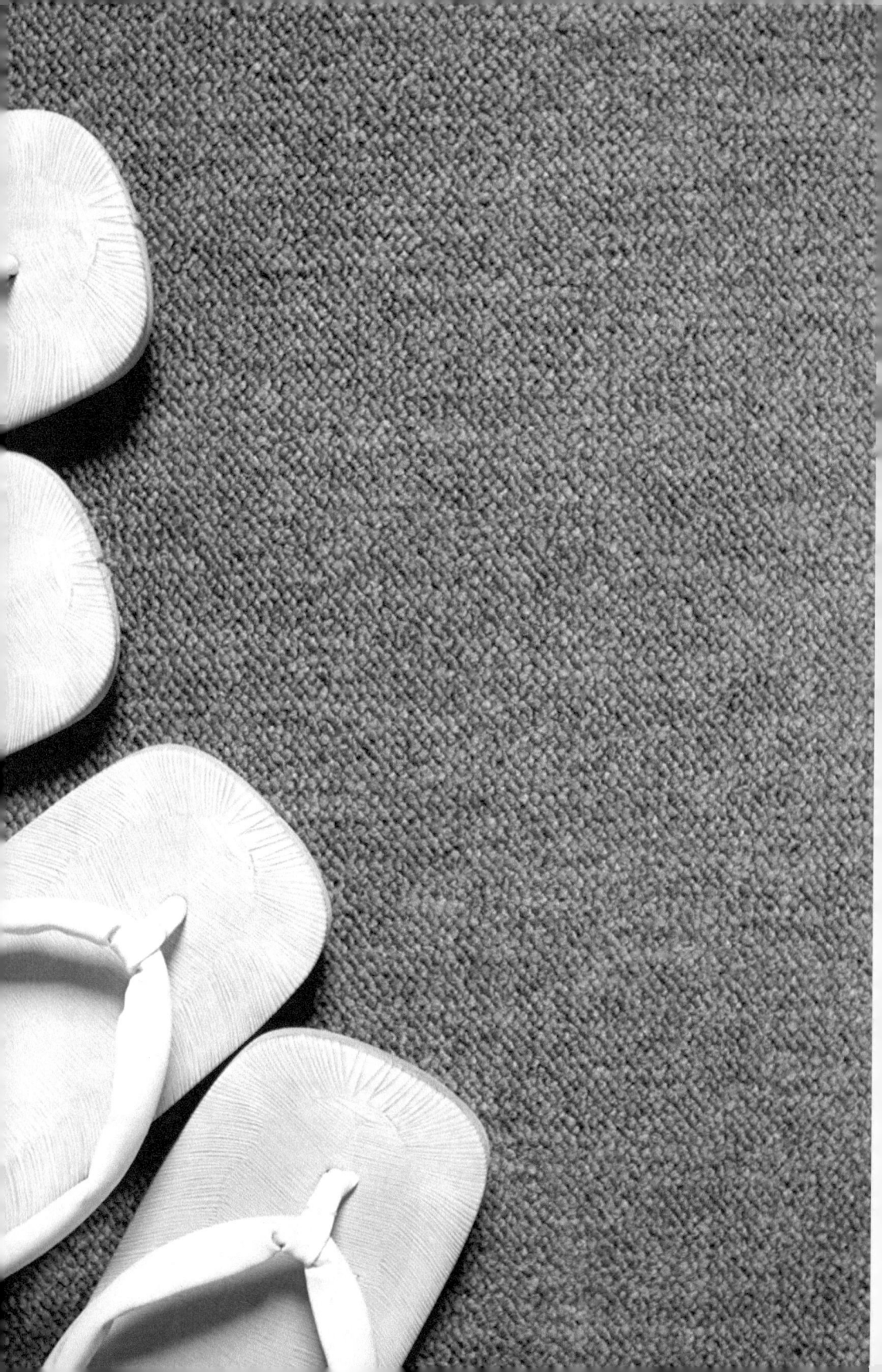

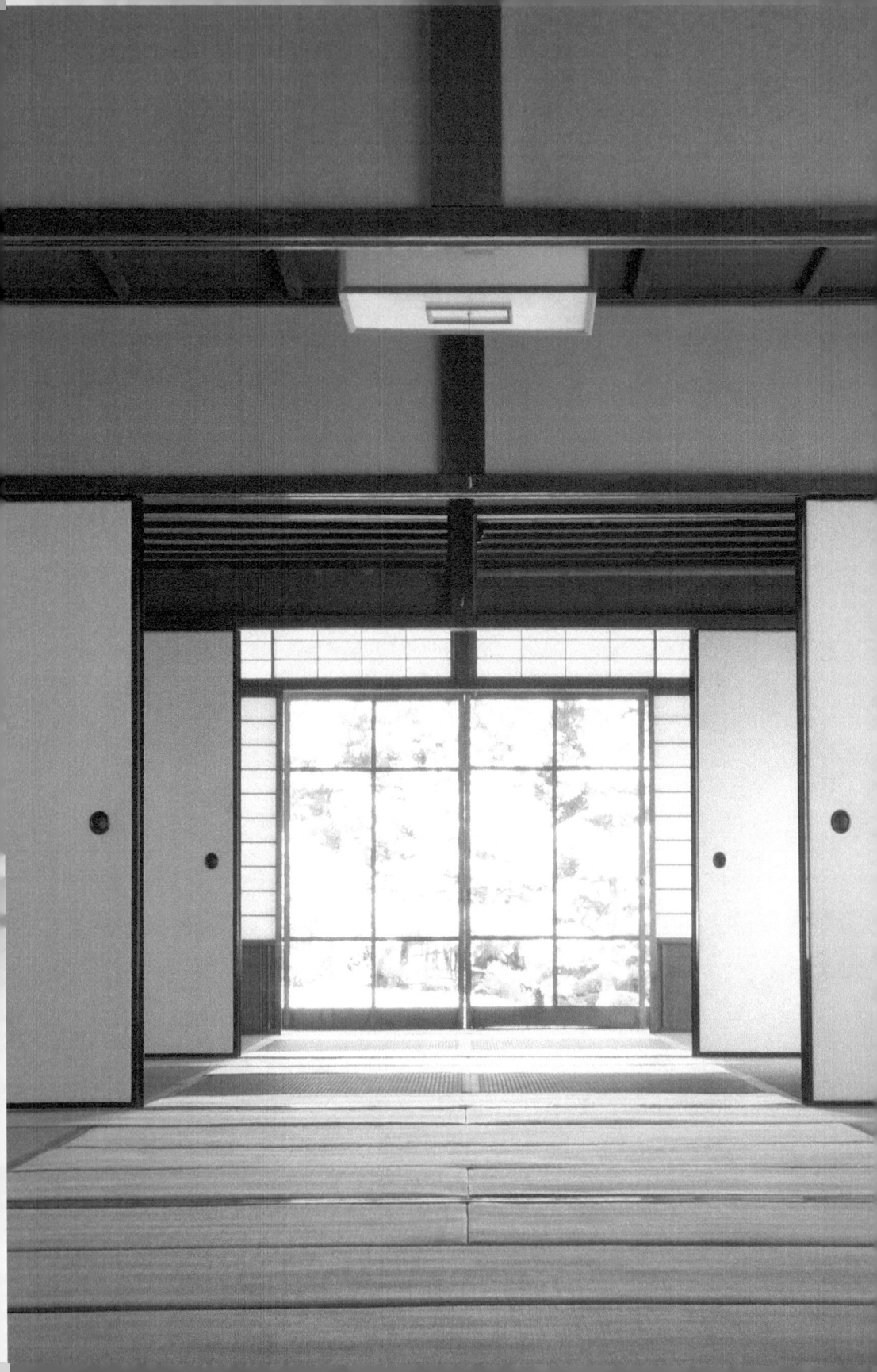

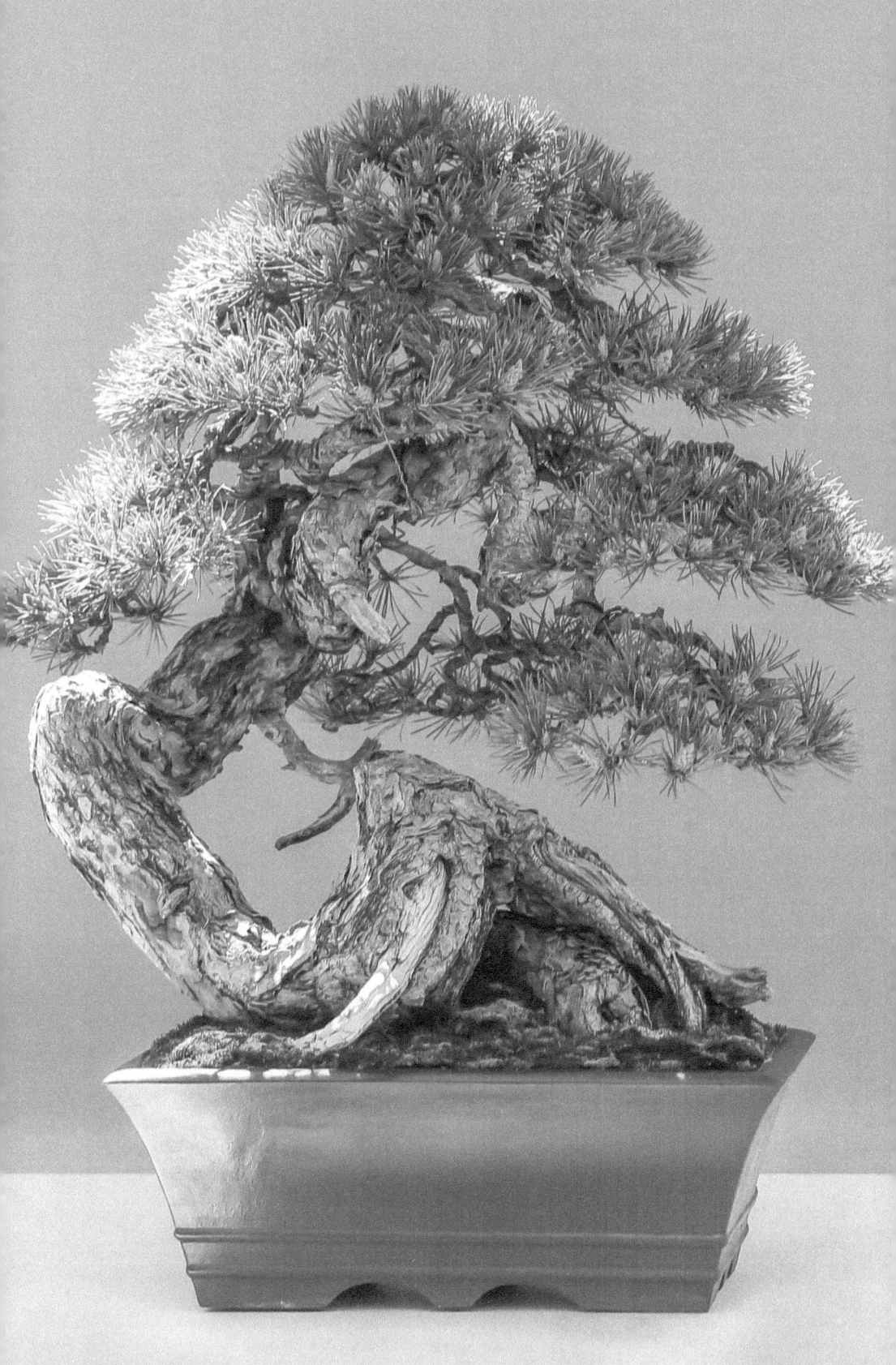

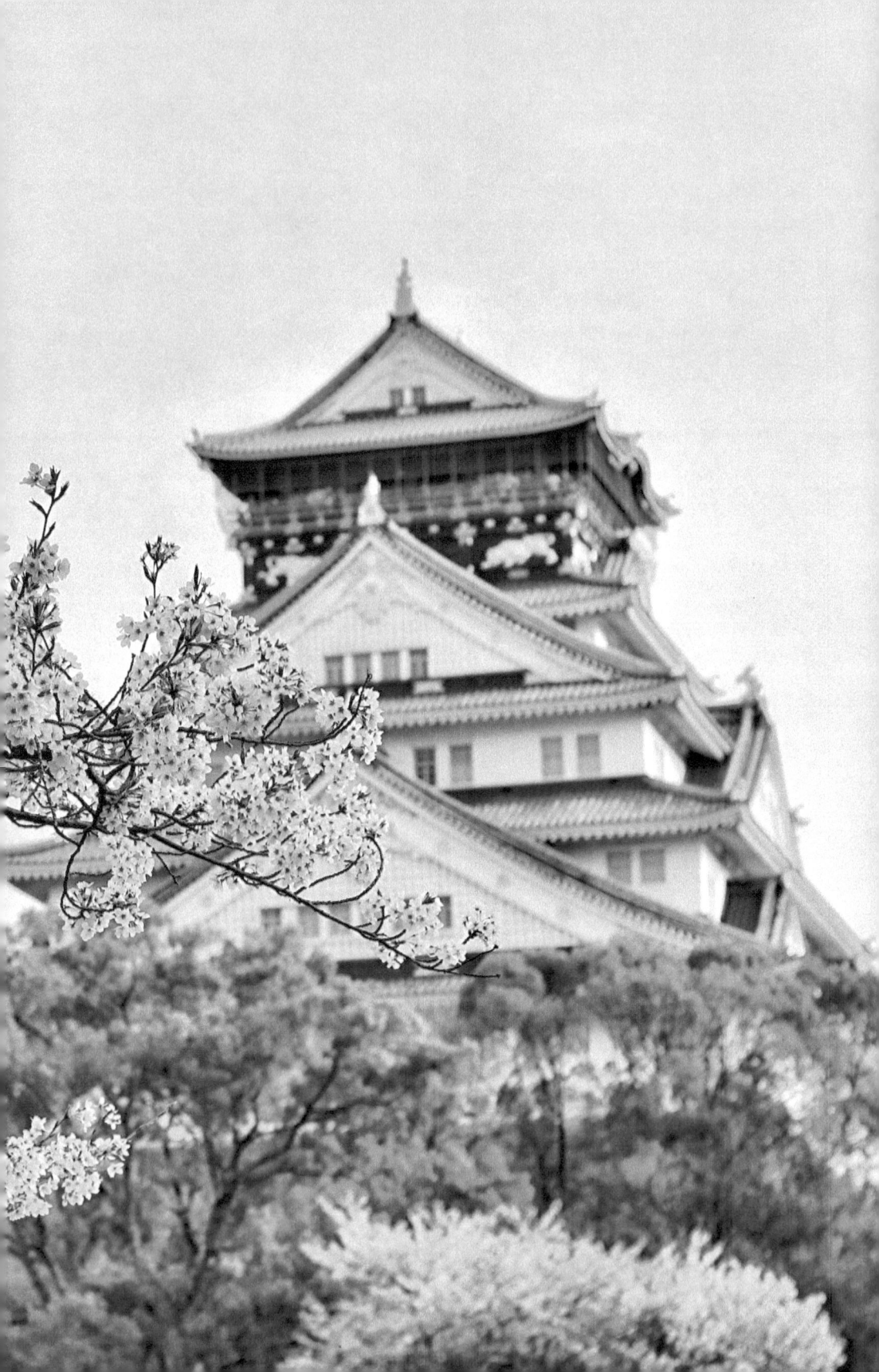

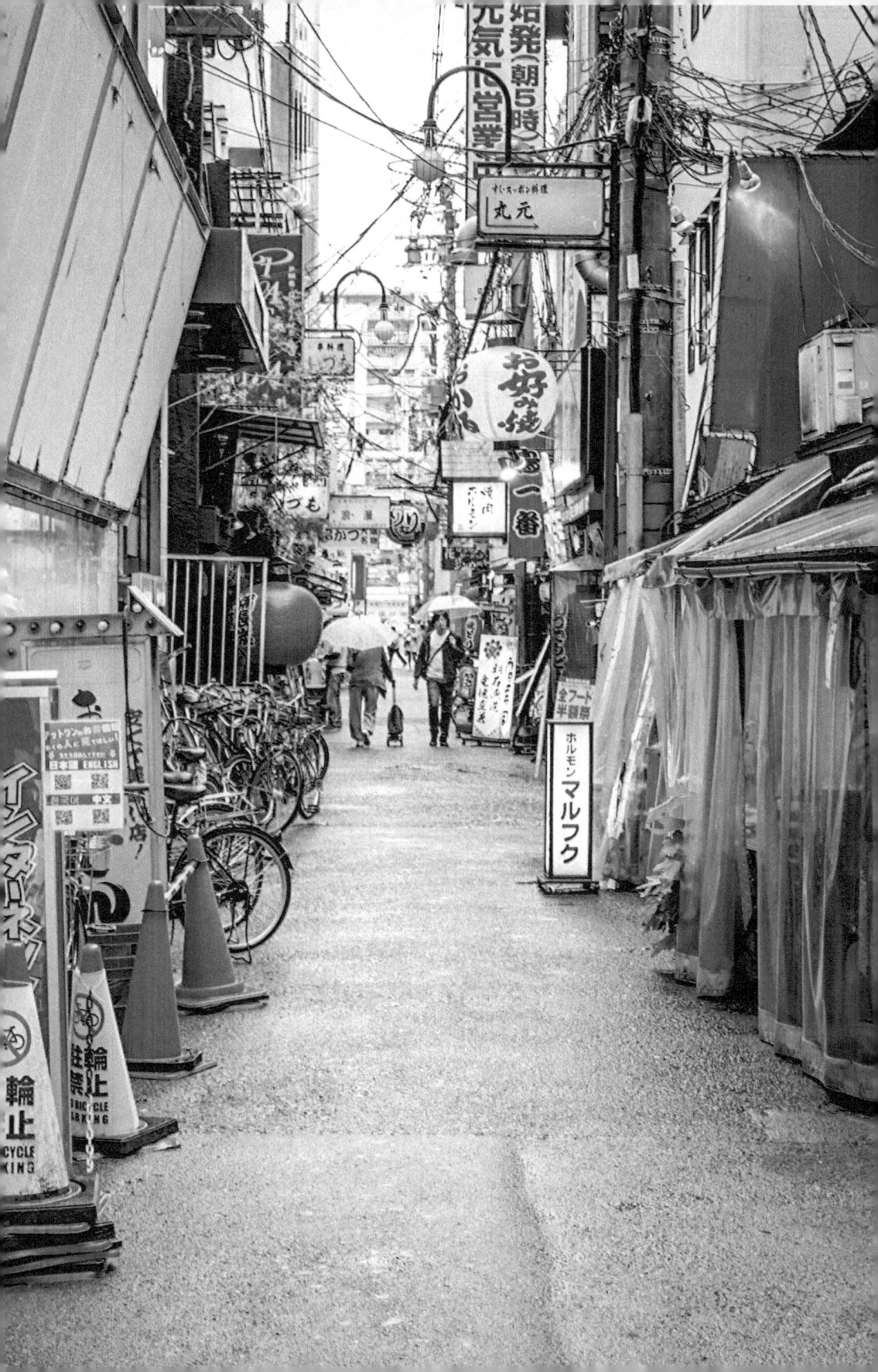

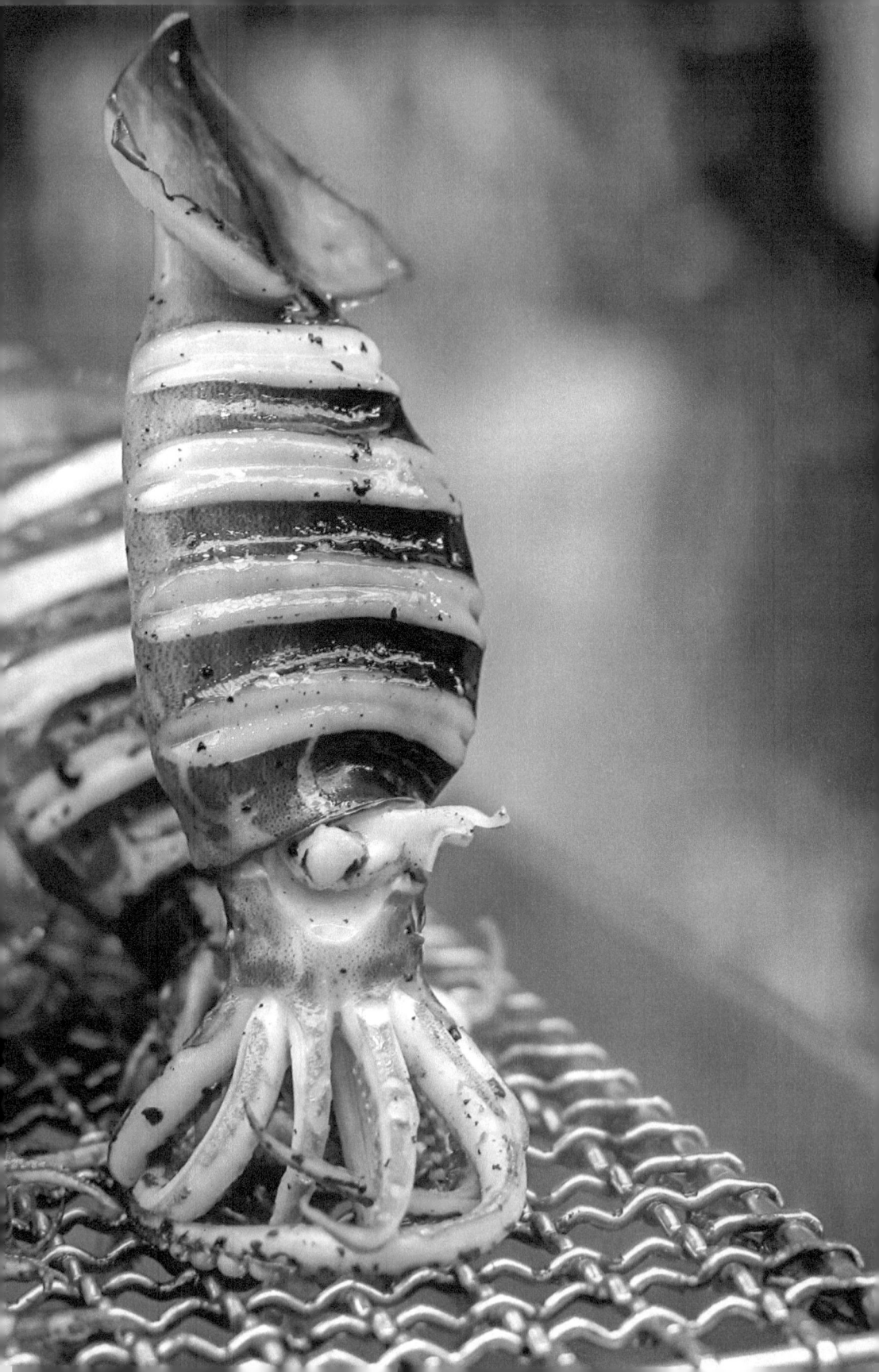

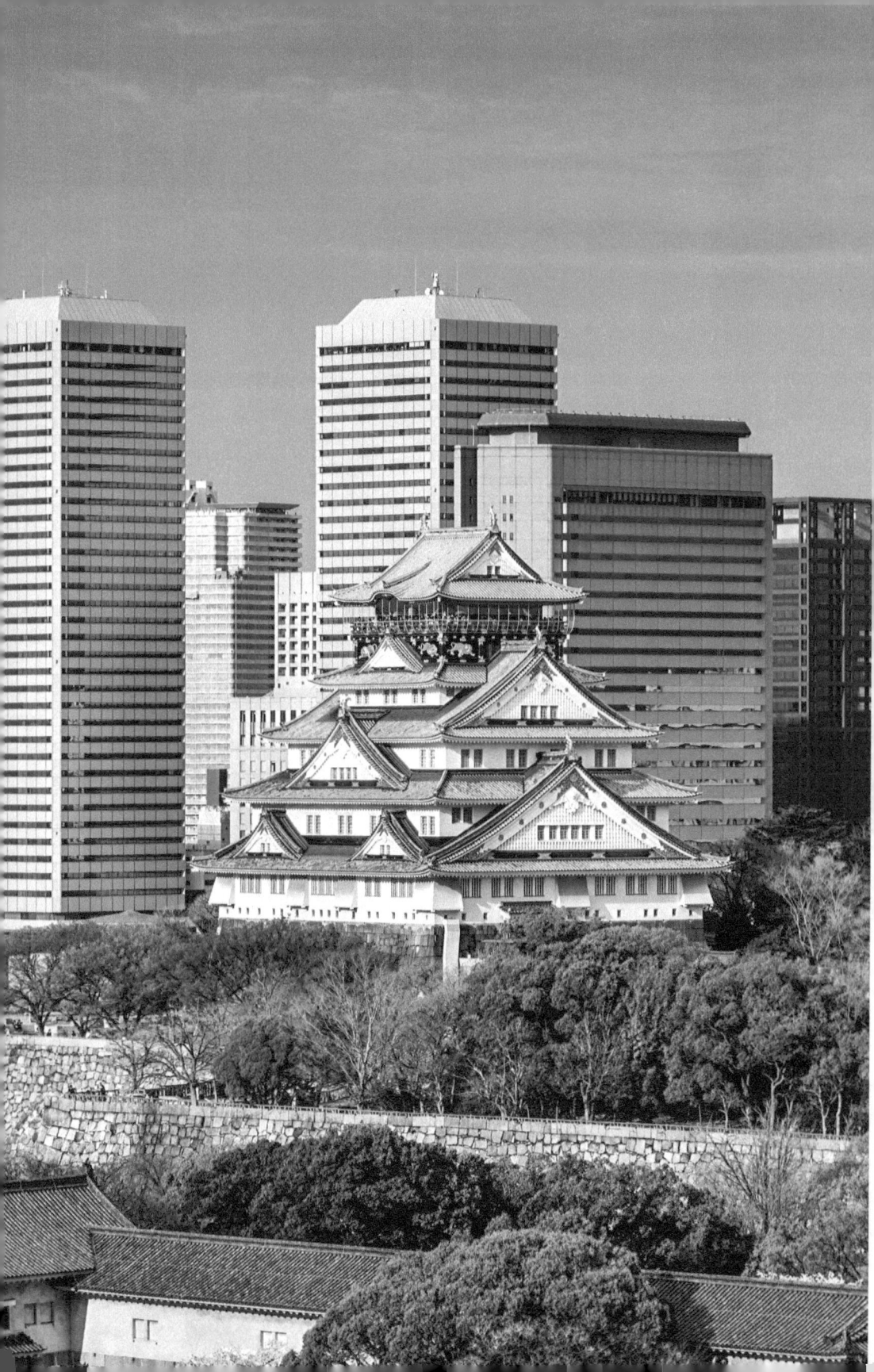

Japanese are one of the most punctual people he had ever worked with. They could, he imagined, put the Germans to shame in their high expectation for timeliness.
Vann Chow

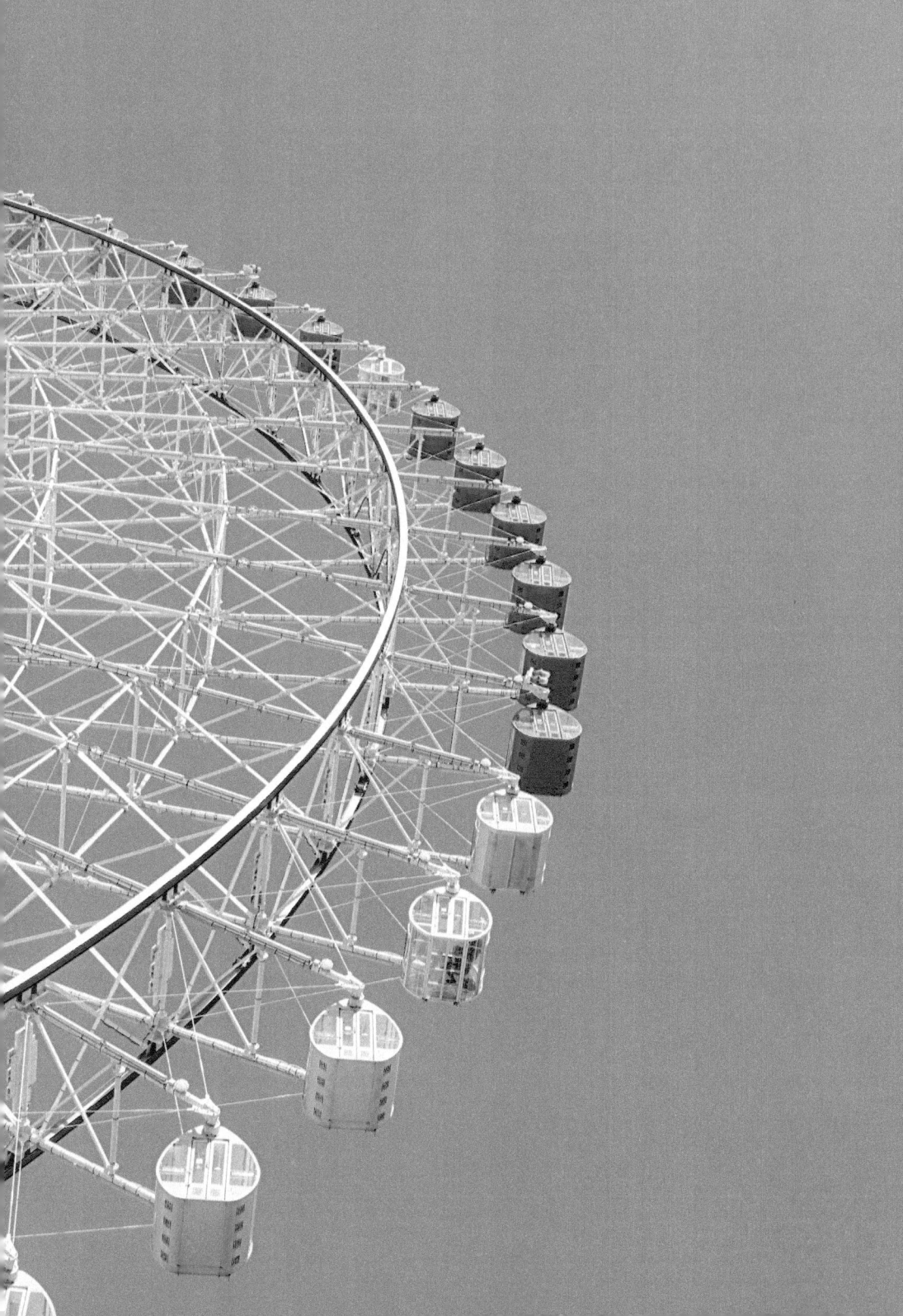

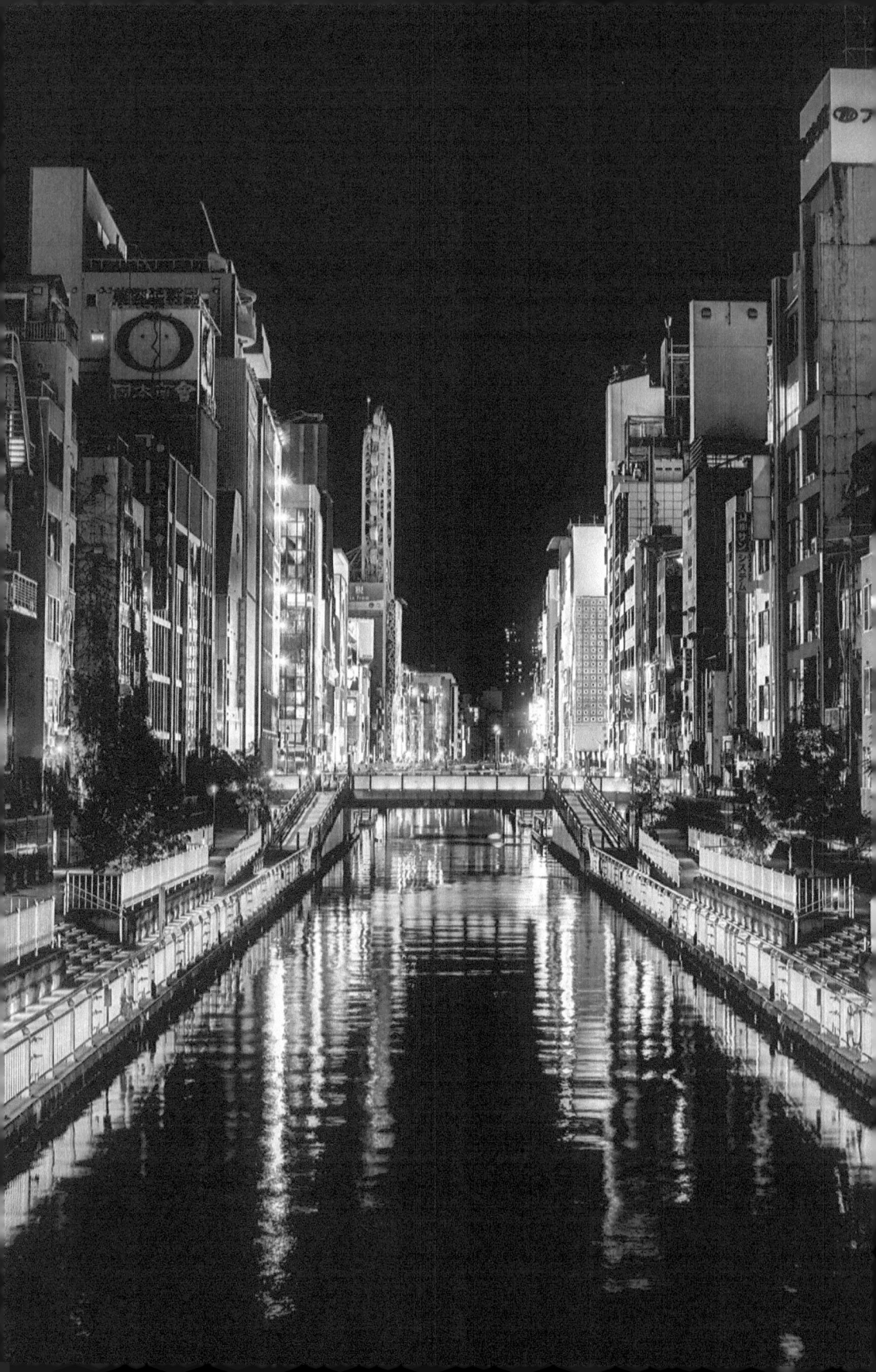

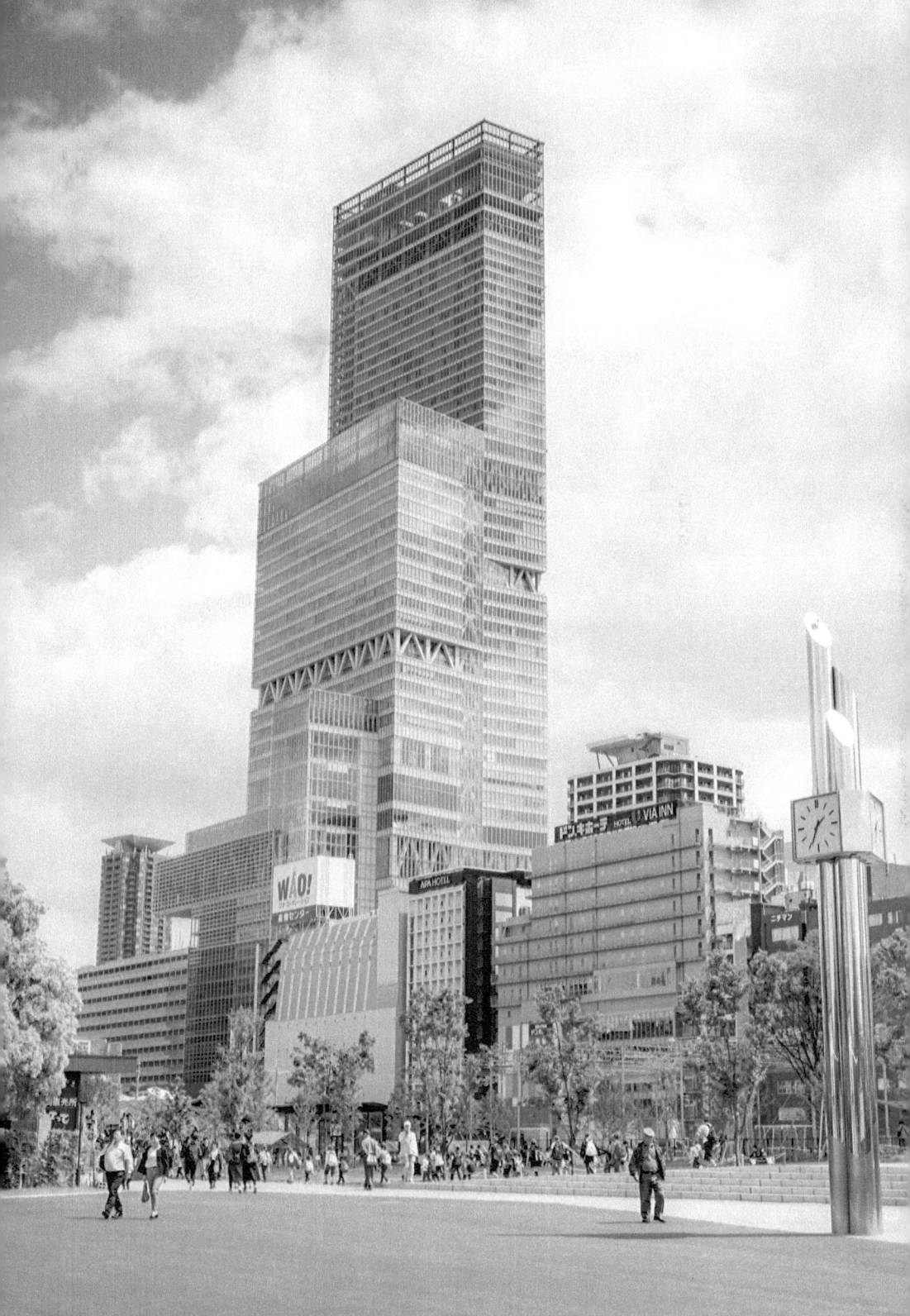

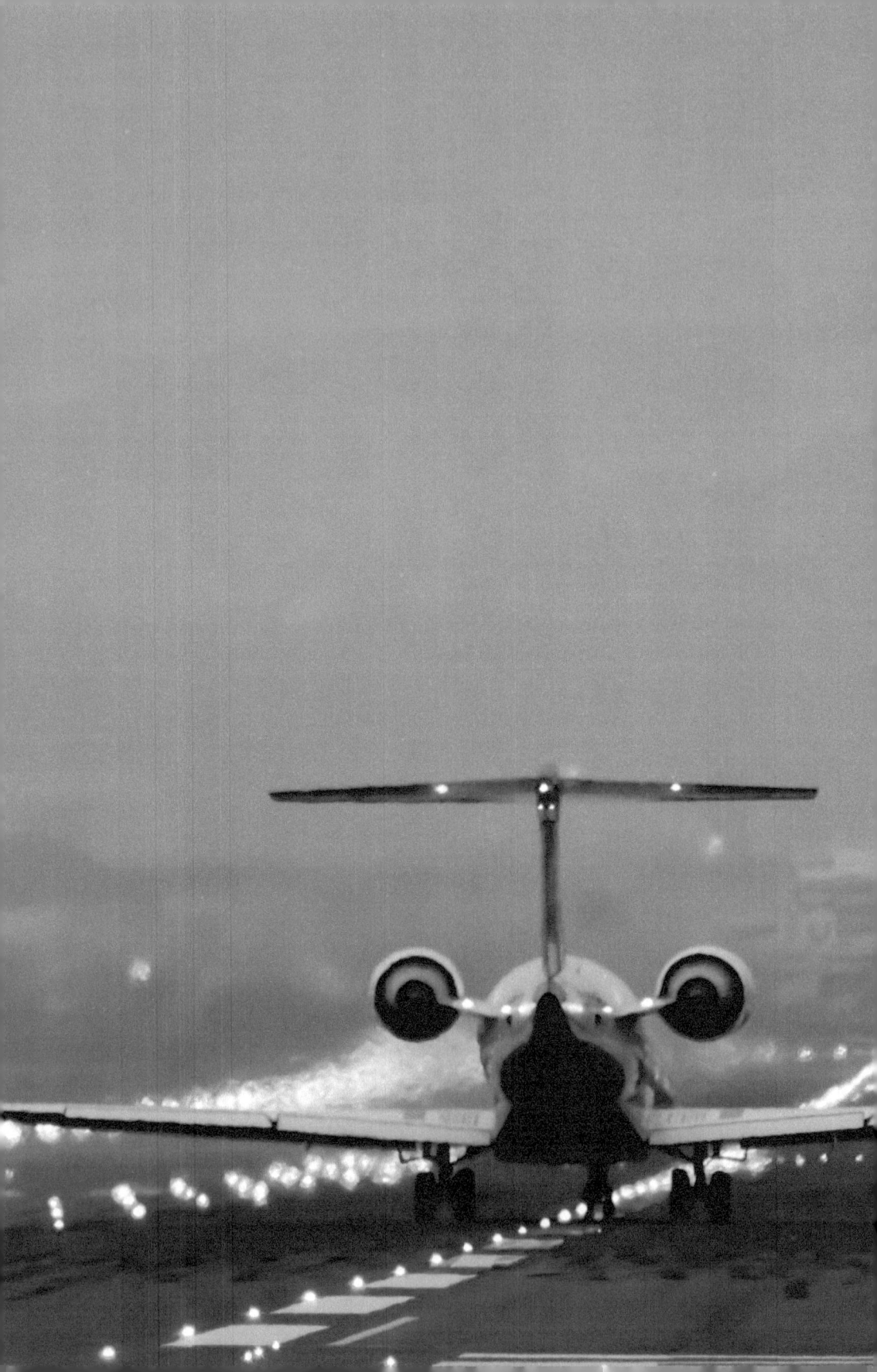

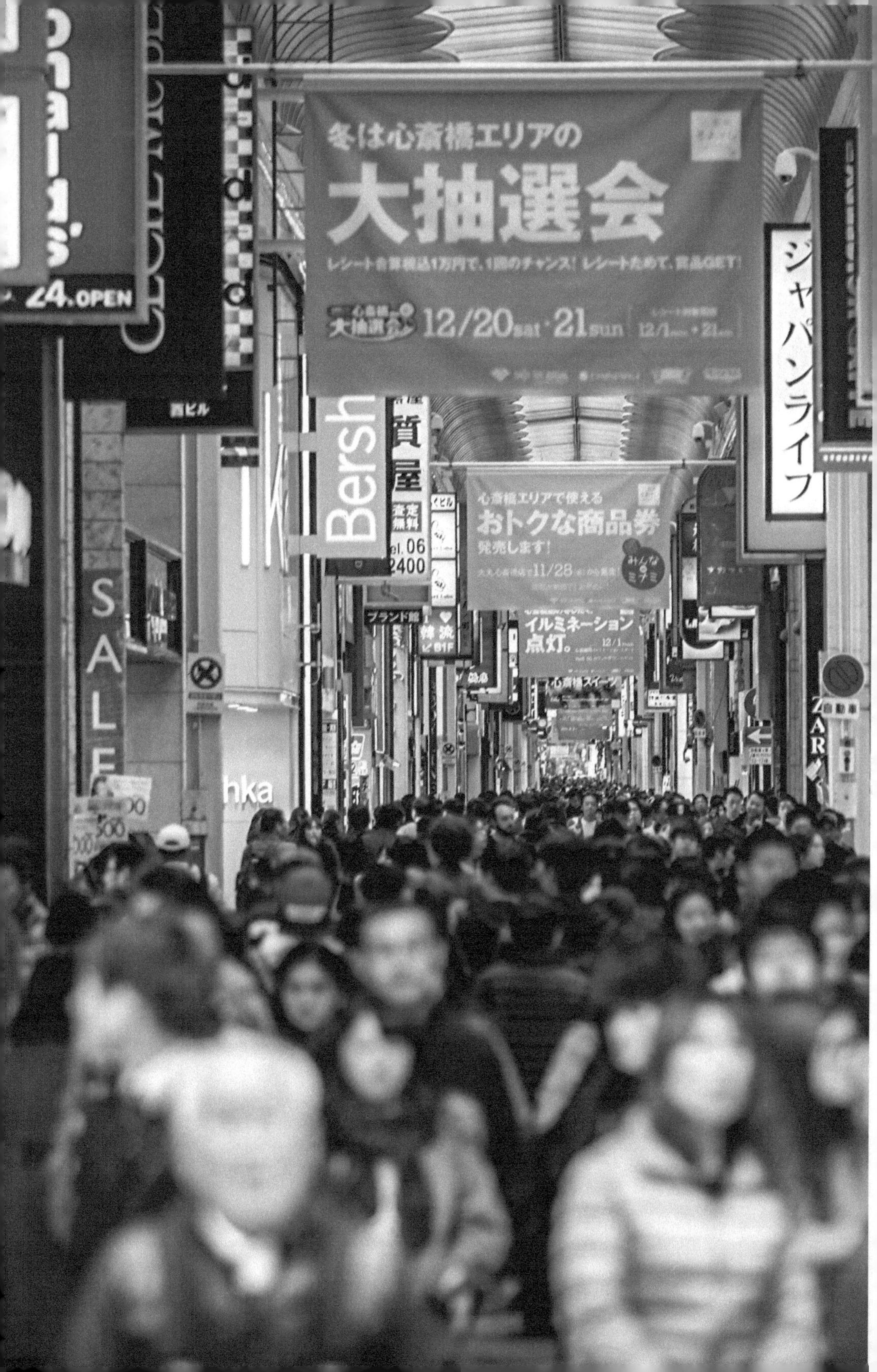
24.OPEN
冬は心斎橋エリアの
大抽選会
12/20sat・21sun
西ビル
Bersh
質屋
ジャパンライフ
心斎橋エリアで使える
おトクな商品券
発売します！
SALE
ブランド館
韓流
イルミネーション
点灯。
hka

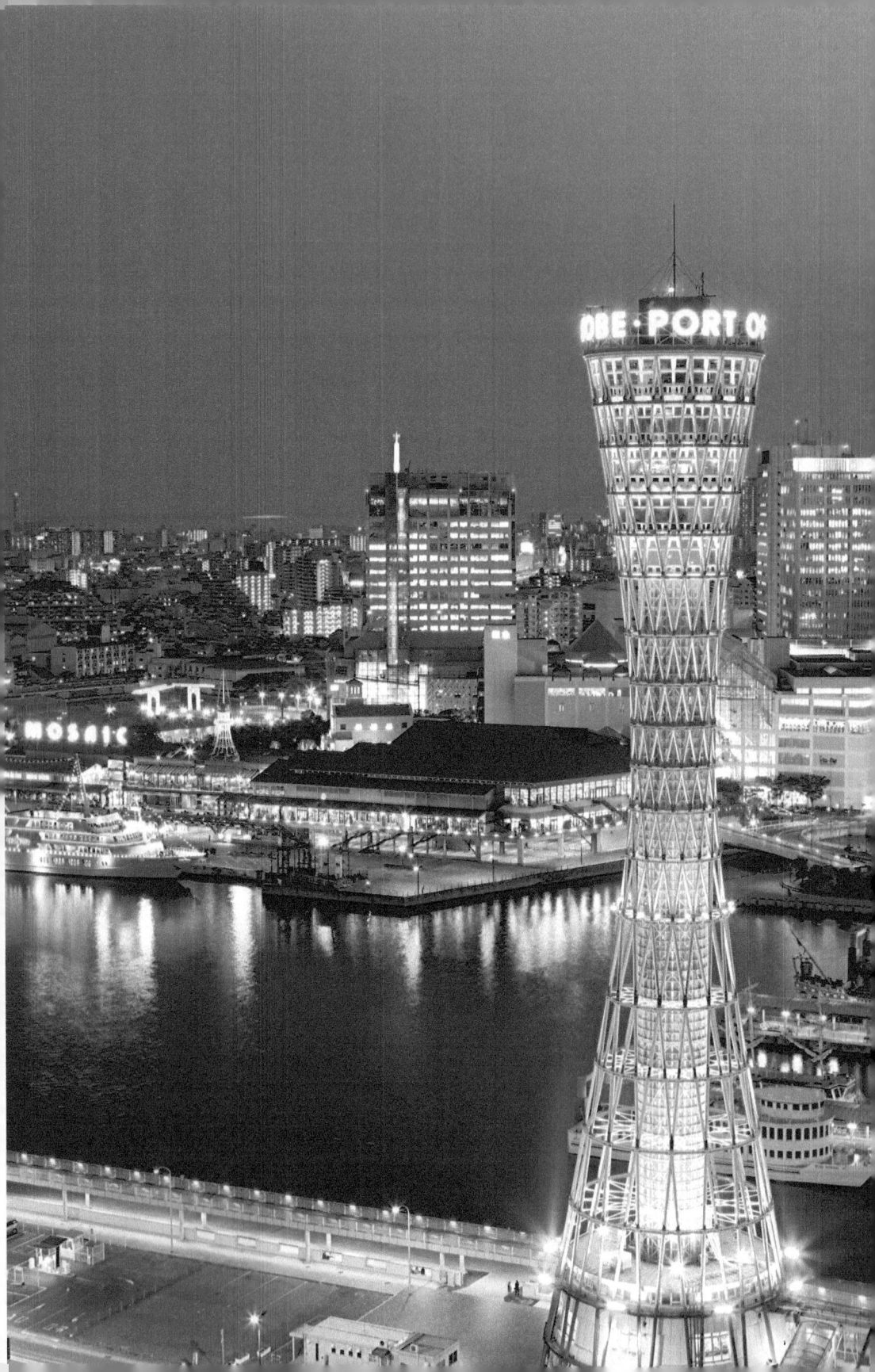

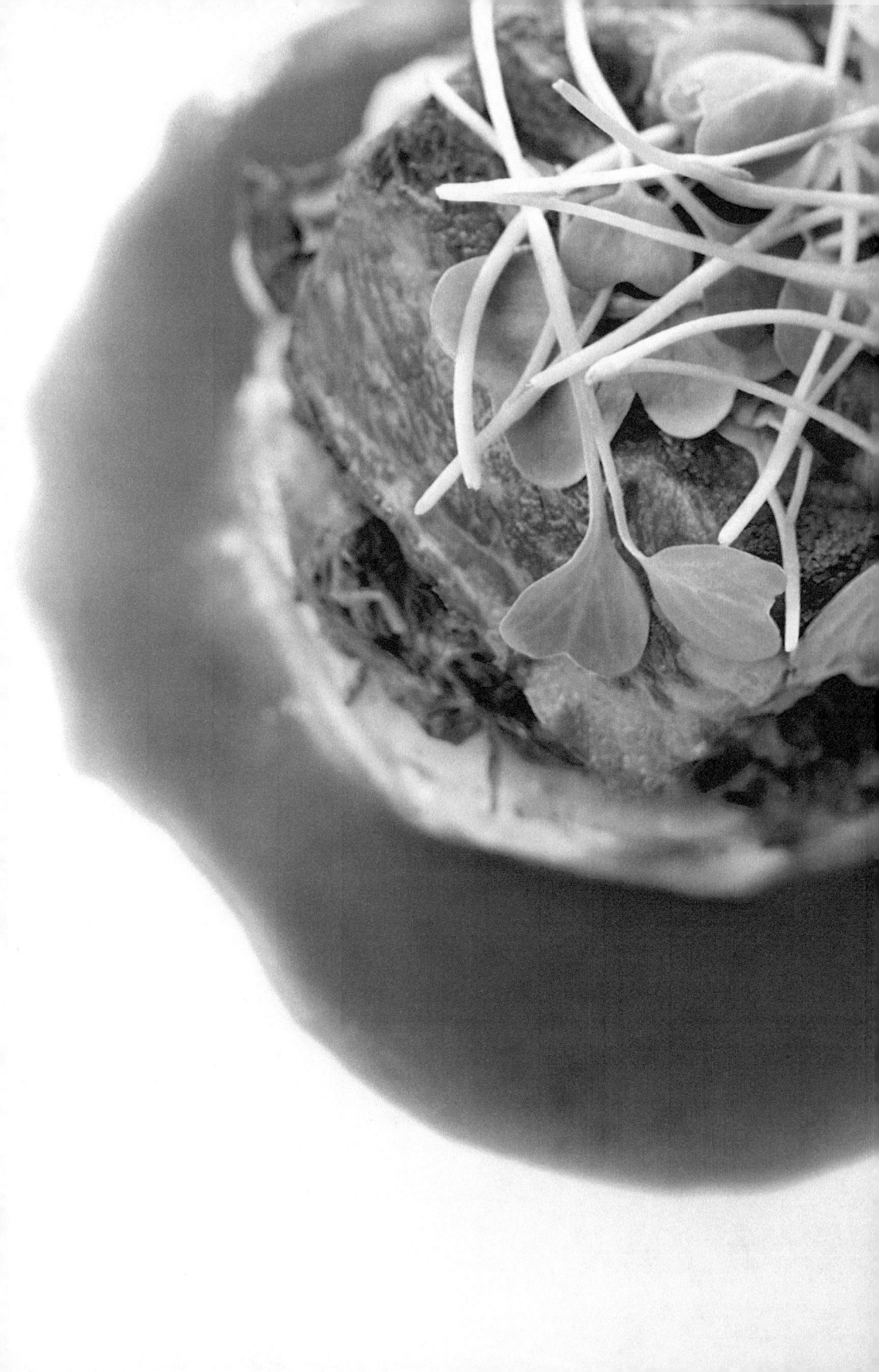

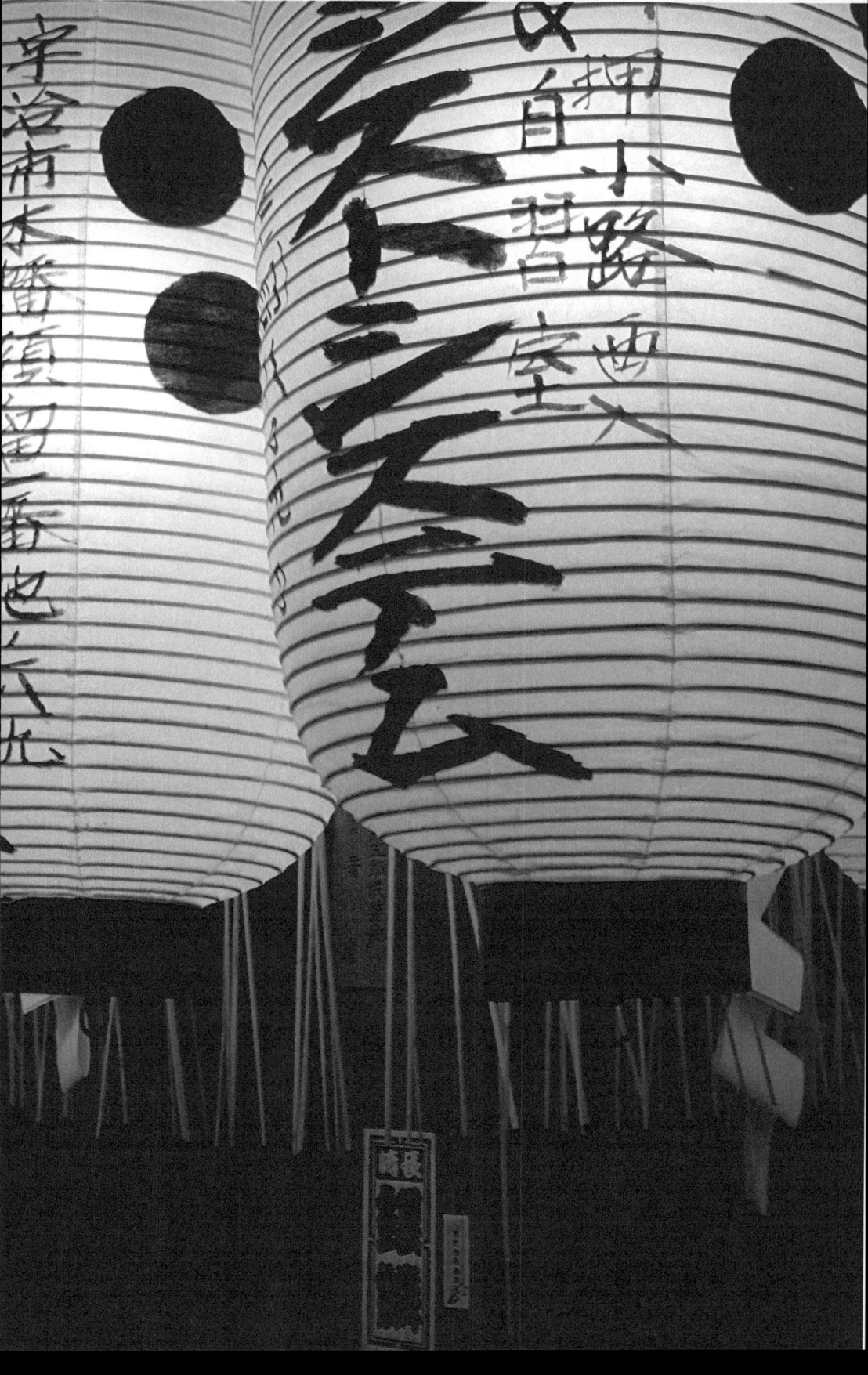

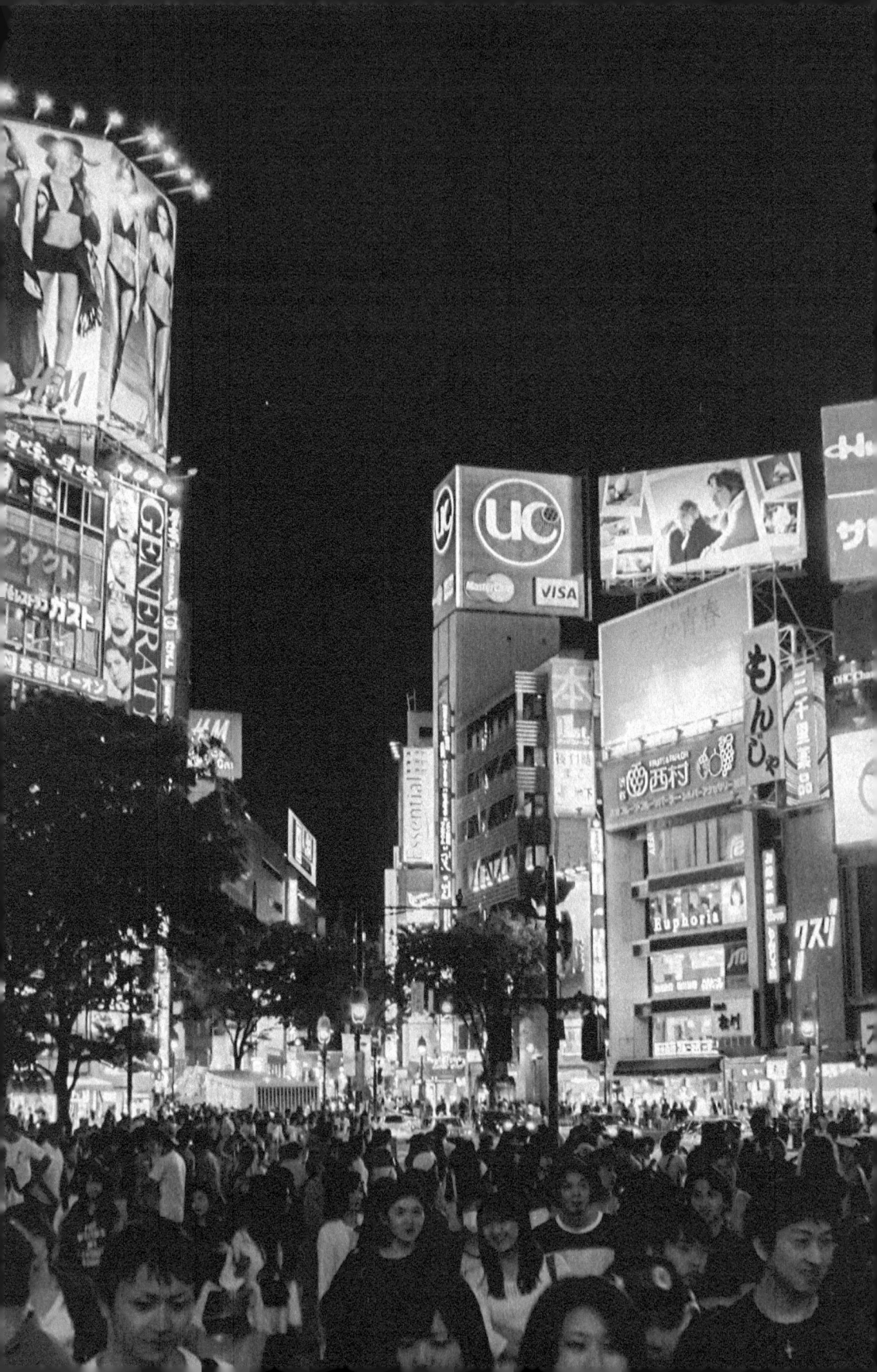

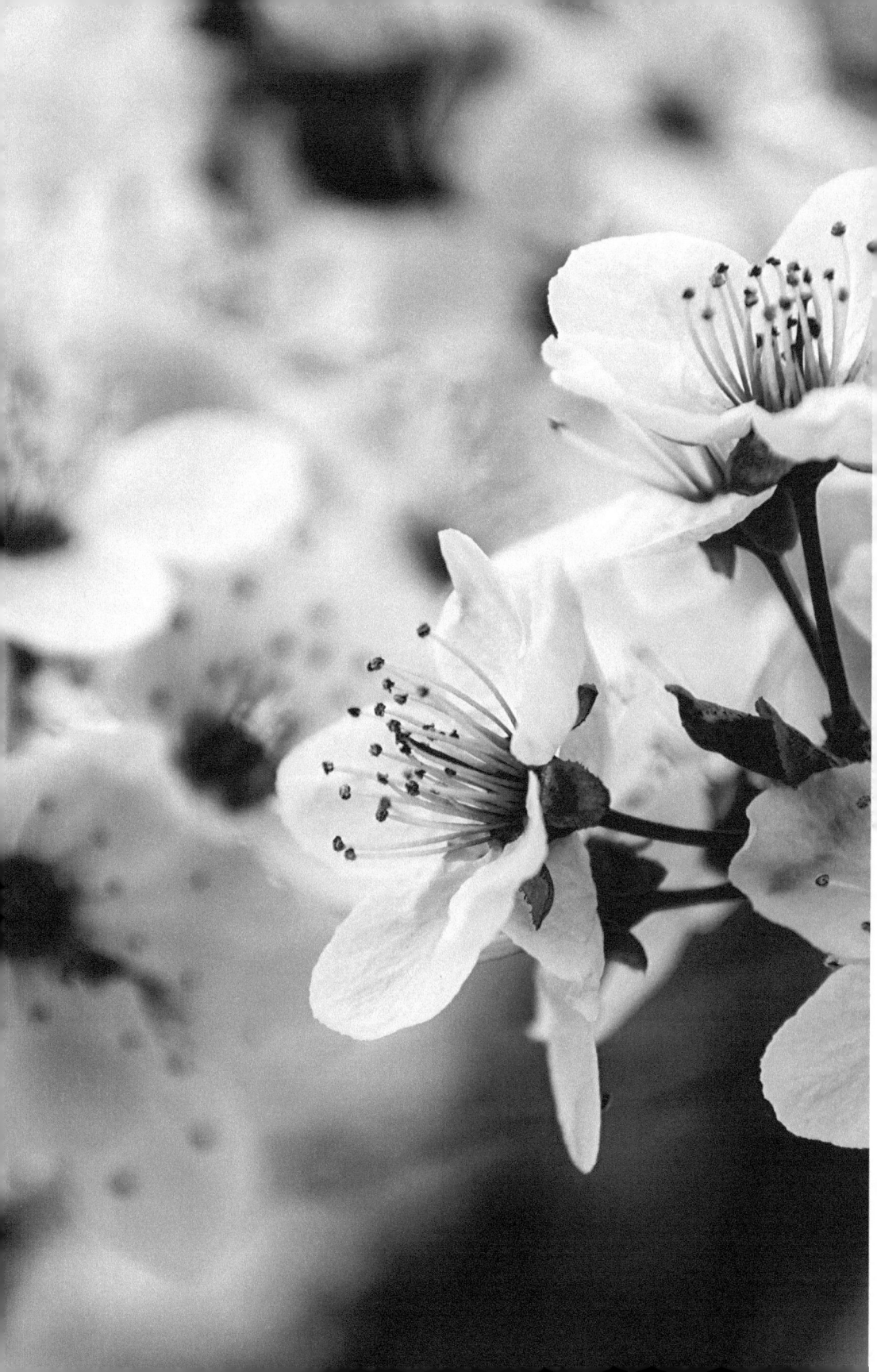

www.ingramcontent.com/pod-product-compliance
Lightning Source LLC
Chambersburg PA
CBHW021038180526
45163CB00005B/2175